500 SERMON OUTLINES

Evangelism

John Ritchie

Kregel
Academic & Professional

500 Evangelistic Sermon Outlines

by John Ritchie

Published in 1987 by Kregel Publications, a division of Kregel, Inc., 2450 Oak Industrial Dr. NE, Grand Rapids, MI 49505.

Library of Congress Cataloging-in-Publication Data
Ritchie, John, 1853–1930.
500 evangelistic sermon outlines / by John Ritchie.
    p. cm.
    Reprint. Originally published: Five Hundred Evangelistic Subjects. Kilmarnock (Strathclyde): Office of the believer's Magazine; London: A. Holness, 1915.
    Continues: Five hundred Gospel subjects, 1904.
    Includes index.
    1. Evangelistic sermons—Outlines, syllabi, etc. I. Title.
BV3793.R48F58   1987   251'.02—dc20   86-27200

ISBN 978-0-8254-3583-6

Printed in the United States of America

5 6 7 8 9 / 24 23 22 21 20 19 18 17 16

CONTENTS

PUBLISHER'S PREFACE

"Preach the Word" was the admonition that Paul gave to the young preacher, Timothy (2 Tim. 4:2). What was so essential 2000 years ago is still necessary today. To "preach the Word" is to expound Scripture truths with clarity and conviction.

The *John Ritchie Sermon Outline* series has helped many to preach effectively since they were first published. Based on Scripture portions, these outlines bring out truths that change lives and minister to present needs. These aids are not intended to diminish a personal, prayerful study of the Bible. Rather, they will encourage it by giving insights to those who preach or teach God's truths.

These brief sermon outlines will enlighten, instruct and give direction to the believer as he walks the path marked out in the Word. They will also refresh and strengthen the inner man in his desire to better know God's word.

For the busy preacher or lay person who needs stimulating ideas for a dynamic preaching or teaching ministry, these sermon outlines will be most beneficial.

THE EVANGELIST AND
HIS MESSAGE

The evangelist, as his name implies, is "a declarer of good tidings." The evangel is "the Gospel of God concerning His Son Jesus Christ, our Lord" (Rom. 1:1-3). And this "Gospel of the glory of the blessed God" (1 Tim. 1:11), has as its purpose and object — the salvation of sinners, here and now. It is to be made known among all the nations (Rom. 1:5), and through its proclamation in this age of grace, and of the Spirit's presence and power on earth, God is taking out of these nations "a people for His Name" (Acts 15:14). When this set time of favor, this "acceptable year of the Lord" (Luke 11:19) reaches its close, the saved will be removed from earth to heaven, grace will cease to reign, and judgment will come upon all who "know not God, and on them that obey not the Gospel of our Lord Jesus" (2 Thess. 1:8). Surely then, it becomes all who know and love this Gospel, and hold this ministry of reconciliation as a sacred trust (1 Thess. 2:4) from God, to be earnest and diligent in making it known, after the apostolic pattern and example, "publicly and from house to house" (Acts 20:20), everywhere and always, "in season, out of season" (2 Tim. 4:2), while ever remembering the Lord's final word — "Go ye into *all* the world and preach the Gospel to *every* creature" (Mark 16:15). That those who heard that Word understood its meaning, and felt its power, is shown in the sequel, for we are told immediately after, that "they went forth and preached *everywhere*, the Lord working with them and confirming the Word" (v. 20).

The Preacher

He, although a "voice" (John 1:23), and in his own estimation as "nothing" (2 Cor. 12:11), is an "ambassador for Christ" (2 Cor. 5:20), standing in His stead, armed with His authority, to proclaim the greatest message mankind will ever hear. He ought to be a "man of God, fully furnished" (2 Tim. 3:17), and always "ready to preach the Gospel" (Rom. 1:15), maintaining a right spiritual condition before God, and a clean and blameless life before men (1 Thess. 2:10). If these are lacking, his preaching, however sound, will be void of power and barren in result.

The Message

The opening verses of First Corinthians 15 give a plain statement of the Gospel as Paul preached it to the people of Corinth, when he entered that city with the holy determination burning in his soul to know nothing among them, cultured and accustomed to the world's wisdom as they were, save "Jesus Christ and Him crucified" (1 Cor. 2:2). Here, he gives the very words in which he preached, as he had received them from the Lord, for he says "I make known, I say, in *what words* I preached it unto you." And these are the very "words": "That Christ died for our sins according to the Scriptures; and that He was buried; and that he rose again the third day according to the Scriptures." We should study the examples of preaching which have been preserved to us in the Word — notably the two great Gospel declarations of Peter and of Paul to Gentile hearers, as recorded in Acts 10 and 13. In a day of "other gospels" which have no Divine message in them to ruined sinners, and no power with them to bring men from the service and power of Satan unto God, it behoves all who go forth with God's evangel, to preach it with no uncertain sound, and to make it known in words which are according to "the Word of the truth of the Gospel" (Col. 1:5).

The Power Which Does the Work

The Apostle Paul tells us that his message at Thessalonica was not "in *word* only, but also in *power* and in the *Holy Spirit*" (1 Thess. 1:5). It was this "demonstration of the Spirit and of power" (1 Cor. 2:4), that he counted on to do the work of convicting and converting sinners. The same power is available today, for although "signs and wonders" are no longer with us, the presence of the Holy Spirit abides, and where He is owned and honored, He never fails to do His work. So that the old Gospel, in its fulness and freshness, faithfully proclaimed, "with the Holy Spirit sent down from heaven" (1 Peter 1:12), is the *message* and the *means* whereby sinners of all nations, and in all conditions, can be reached and converted to God.

Let the preacher make it his first and chief concern to present himself a clean and sanctified vessel, "meet for the Master's use," having the Word of Christ dwelling richly in his own soul. Let all service be *for* God, be preceded by seasons of waiting *upon* God, to hear His voice, to receive His message, and to be assured of His guidance. And let only such means be used in making known the message as are worthy of God. Let the Lord's servant preach seeking only to please the One whom He serves, and without fear of man of seeking flattery from him, let him preach Christ, in a Christlike spirit, for Christ's sake, and God will see to the results here and to his full reward hereafter.

EVANGELISTIC MESSAGES

1   The Gospel

The Gospel of the Grace of God (Acts 20:24)
The Gospel of the Glory of Christ (2 Cor. 4:4)
The Gospel of our Salvation (Eph. 1:13)

     1. Its character and its message
     2. The subject and its object
     3. Its purpose and its power

2   The Death of Christ

It was a Propitiation (Rom. 3:23)
It was a Peacemaking (Col. 1:20)
It was a Purchase (Acts 20:28)

     1. This is Godward, and for all (1 John 4:10)
     2. Once for all made, now proclaimed (Rom. 10:15)
     3. He purchased in order to possess (Titus 2:14)

3   Salvation

Acquired by Christ's Atonement (Heb. 2:9)
Assured by Christ's Resurrection (Rom. 5:10)
Proclaimed in the Gospel Message (Acts 13:26)
Possessed by faith in Christ (Acts 16:31)

     The Cross, its procuring cause (1 Peter 3:18)
     The Living Lord, its assuring source (John 13:19)
     The Gospel, its Word of power (Rom. 1:16)
     Faith, its receiving hand (Eph. 2:8)

4 Forgiveness of Sins

Christ died to procure it (Col. 1:14)
Christ lives to impart it (Acts 5:31)
The Gospel freely proclaims it (Acts 13:38)
The believing sinner possesses it (1 John 2:12)

5 A Great Savior

(John 1:14)

Incarnation—"The Word became flesh"
Humiliation—"And tabernacled among us"
Salvation—"Full of Grace and Truth"

The Deity, manhood, perfect life and atoning death of Christ are all involved and engaged in the sinner's salvation. To reject or deny either, is to lose all.

6 A Confessed Christianity

(Psalm 40:10)

God's Righteousness Proclaimed (Rom. 1:17; 3:25)
God's Salvation Declared (Acts 28:28)
God's Loving-kindness Manifested (Isa. 63:7)

Faith receives God's righteousness (Rom. 1:16)
Confession is made of His salvation (Rom. 10:9)
Testimony is given of His kindness (Titus 3:4)

7 Facts for Everybody

(John 3:14-16)

A Great *Need*—Man ruined (Rom. 5:12)
A Grand *Provision*—Christ uplifted (Rom. 5:8)
A General *Invitation*—No exceptions (Acts 10:44)
A Glorious *Assurance*—No doubts (John 10:28)

8 God's Salvation

Is Common to all who believe (Jude 3)
Is Great, because of what it saves from (Heb. 2:3)
Is Eternal, because of who brought it (Heb. 9:12)

The *First* tells it is *for* all nations (Rom. 1:5)
The *Second* avers it is *from* all iniquity (Titus 2:14)
The *Third* asserts it is *unto* all eternity (Heb. 7:25)

9   Salvation's Securities

The Work of Christ procures Salvation (Heb 9:12)
The Word of God assures Salvation (Acts 16:31)
Witness of the Spirit secures Salvation (Eph. 4:30)
> The Work of the Cross is unchangeable (Heb. 10:12)
> The Word of God is unbreakable (1 Peter 1:25)
> The Witness of the Spirit is unanswerable (Rom. 8:15)

10   The Cross of Christ

The Darkest Exhibition of Man's Sin (Acts 4:27, 28)
Brightest Display of God's Love (1 John 3:10)
The Greatest Witness of Satan's Defeat (Heb. 2:14)
The Mightiest Work for Man's Salvation (1 Cor. 1:18)

11   Faith in Exercise

Justified by Faith (Rom. 5:1)—Our Release
Saved through Faith (Eph. 2:8)—Our Deliverance
Sanctified by Faith (Acts 26:18)—Our Position
Purified by Faith (Acts 15:9)—Our Condition

12   Three Great Gospel Blessings

Imputed Righteousness (Rom. 4:22-24)
Imparted Life (1 John 5:11-13)
Implanted Nature (2 Peter 1:3-4)
> The *First* is ours in virtue of the Cross (Rom. 5:1)
> The *Second* is from the living Christ in Heaven (Col. 3:3)
> The *Third* is by the Spirit and the Word (1 Peter 1:22, 23)

13   Three Cardinal Truths

Redeemed by the Blood of Christ (1 Peter 1:19)
Regenerated by the Spirit of God (John 3:6)
Renewed by the Word of God (2 Cor. 4:16)
> The *First*, meets our need as slaves of sin
> The *Second*, as sons of Adam
> The *Third*, as children of God

14   Position, Path, and Prospects
Philippians, Chapter 3
Found in Christ (v. 9)—The Believer's Salvation
To Know Christ (v. 10)—The Believer's Object
To Look for Christ (v. 20)—the Believer's Hope

15   Christ's Lordship
Lord of All (Acts 10:36)—By Purchase
Lord of Sinners (2 Peter 2:1)—By Claim
Lord of Saints (Rom. 10:9)—By Confession
Lord of Servants (John 13:13)—By Obedience

16   The Sinner and the Savior
Sinners, He came to *save* (1 Tim. 1:15)
Sinners, He *died* for (Rom. 5:8)
Sinners, He came to *call* (Matt. 9:13)
Sinners, He *receives* (Luke 15:2)

17   Christ and the Law:
His Threefold Work
To Fulfil the Law (Matt. 5:17)—in His Life
To Bear its Curse (Gal. 3:13)—on His Cross
To Redeem from its Power (Gal. 4:5)—by His Death
> By the *First*, He magnified it (Isa. 42:21)
> In the *Second*, He silenced it (Gal. 3:24)
> Through the *Third*, He satisfied it (Rom. 7:4)

18   Things Which Are Prepared
Salvation for the Sinner (Luke 2:30, 31)
Satisfaction for the Believer (Ps. 23:5)
Blessings for the Spiritual (1 Cor. 2:9, 10)
A Place for the Glorified (John 14:2)
> The *First*, is provided by the Cross (1 Cor. 1:18)
> The *Second*, by the living Shepherd (Heb. 13:20)
> The *Third*, is revealed by the Spirit (John 16:13)
> The *Fourth*, awaits us in Heaven (Heb. 11:16)

19 Blessings Received in Christ's Name

Forgiveness is proclaimed in it (Acts 13:38)
Remission is made known through it (Acts 10:43)
Regeneration comes through faith in it (John 1:12)
Life is received by believing in it (John 20:31)
Salvation is found in it alone (Acts 4:12)

20 What God Hath Made

Sinners who believe in His Son

Made righteous in Christ (2 Cor. 5:21)
Made nigh by the Blood (Eph. 2:13)
Made meet for Heaven (Col. 1:12)
Made accepted in the Beloved (Eph. 1:6)

21 The Gospel Call

Called unto Eternal Life (1 Tim. 4:12)
Called into Marvellous Light (1 Peter 2:9)
Called to Holy Liberty (Gal. 5:13)
Called to Eternal Glory (1 Peter 5:10)

22 The Sinner's Confessions

Confession of Sin under Conviction (Ps. 32:5)
Confession of Faith in Christ's Person (John 6:69)
Confession of Christ unto Salvation (Rom. 10:9)

23 Christ and His Sheep

He Purchased them (Acts 20:28)—at the Cross
Seeks and Saves them (Luke 15:4, 5)—by the Gospel
Knows and Marks them (John 10:14, 27)—by His Spirit
Feeds and Leads (Ps. 23:2, 3)—through His Word

24 The New Birth

The Agent—The Spirit of God (John 3:5)
The Instrument—The Word of God (1 Peter 1:23)
The Means—Receiving Christ (John 1:12-14)
The Evidence—Love to God (John 3:5)

25   Three Stages of Christian Life

Deliverance from the Service of Satan (Col. 1:13)
Discipleship to the Lord Jesus (Matt. 28:19)
Delight in the Service of the Lord (Isa. 58:13, 14)

> The *First* is Enjoyed when Christ is Received
> The *Second* is Manifested when Christ is Confessed
> The *Third* is Assured when Christ is Obeyed

26   Salvation, Sanctification, Service

Salvation, the believer's rescue *by* God (Rom. 1:16)
Sanctification is his setting apart *for* God (Heb. 10:12)
Service is his devotion *to* God (Rom. 12:1)

> Salvation is Emancipation from Sin's *Practice*
> Sanctification is Separation from Sin's *Pollution*
> Service is Subjection to God's *Plan*

27   Christ's Threefold Work

By His Atonement on the Cross, we are Justified
By His Advocacy on the Throne, we are Preserved
At His Advent to the Clouds, we shall be Glorified

> For the *First*, see Rom. 5:9; Heb. 9:12
> For the *Second*, see Rom. 5:10; Jude 1
> For the *Third*, see 1 Thess. 4:14-16; 1 John 3:2

28   Our Great Deliverer

He Delivers Sinners from Sin's Bondage (Luke 4:18)
He Rescues from the Power of Darkness (Col. 1:13)
He Severs from the present evil World (Gal. 1:4)
He Delivers from every evil Work (2 Tim. 4:18)

29   Forgiveness of Sins

Its Freeness—By Grace (Rom. 3:24)
Its Fulness—All Trespasses (Col. 2:13)
Its Certainty—"Hath Forgiven" (Eph. 4:32)
Its Eternity—Not Remembered (Heb. 10:17)

30   Dead to God

Professors with a Name to live (Rev. 3:1)
Pleasure-seekers in the World (1 Tim. 5:6)
Prodigals in the far Country (Luke 15:24)

31   Three Great Facts

"It is Written" (Rom. 3:10)—Sinner's Condemnation
"It is Finished" (John 19:30)—Savior's Atonement
"It is I" (Matt. 14:27)—The Saint's Succorer

32   Christ in the Psalms

His Incarnation and Mission (Ps. 40:7)
His Crucifixion and Death (Ps. 22:1, 16)
His Resurrection and Ascension (Ps. 16:9-11)
His Coming again in Glory (Ps. 50:1-3)

33   The Sinner's Ruin

By Nature, a Child of Wrath (Eph. 2:3)
By Practice, a Wanderer from God (Isa. 53:6)
In Mind, an Enemy toward God (Rom. 8:7)
In Guilt, a Criminal before God (Rom. 3:19)

34   Profession, Possession, Confession

Profession, without Reality (Titus 1:12)
Possession, with Enjoyment (1 John 5:9)
Confession, result of Faith (Rom. 10:9)

> Profession, without Possession, is Hypocrisy (Luke 12:46)
> Possession, without Confession, is Cowardice (John 12:42)
> Confession is God's Way of Blessing to others (John 6:69)

35   Three Typical Miracles of the Lord

Recovered from Disease (Mark 1:31)
Rescued from Demons (Mark 9:25-27)
Raised from Death (Mark 5:41)

> All three are effected in the Sinner's Conversion:
> He is Healed by His Stripes (Isa. 53:5)
> He is Delivered by His Power (Col. 1:13)
> He has Life as His Gift (John 10:28)

36   Subjects for Thanksgivings

For God's Unspeakable Gift (2 Cor. 9:19)
For Deliverance from Sin's Slavery (Rom. 6:17)
For Fitness to be in Heaven (Col. 1:12)

The Gift received, gives the Deliverance desired, and "in Christ" the meetness for Heaven is obtained.

37   The Word of God

Begets, when Received (James 1:18)
Purifies, when Obeyed (1 Peter 1:22)
Feeds, when Desired (1 Peter 2:2)
Judges, when Rejected (Matt. 12:48)

The Instrument of the Spirit in Regeneration (John 3:5)
The Message which effects Sanctification (John 17:17)
The Means which promotes Edification (Jude 20)
The Standard which will be used in Condemnation (John 12:48)

38   Full Salvation

As Typified in Israel's History

The Passover (Exod. 12)—Shelter from Judgment
The Red Sea (Exod. 14)—Deliverance from Sin
The River Jordan (Josh. 2)—In Christ: in Heaven

The *First* is by Faith in the Blood of Christ (Rom. 3:25)
The *Second* is through Participation in His Death (Col. 1:13)
The *Third* is in Death and Resurrection with Him (Eph. 2:5, 6)

39   The Power of Christ

Proved by Creation (Col. 1:15-18)
Manifested in Salvation (1 Cor. 1:24)
Experienced in Preservation (2 Tim. 1:12)
Enjoyed in Weakness (2 Cor. 12:9)

40   The Power of the Spirit

Exercised in the Sinner's Conviction (John 16:8)
Manifested in the Believer's Conversion (1 Thess. 1:5)
Employed in the Saint's Strengthening (Eph. 3:16)
Bestowed in the Servant's Qualification (Acts 1:8)

41 Jesus Christ, the Savior

His Coming and His Mission (1 Tim. 1:15)
His Death and its Object (1 Peter 3:18)
His Life and its Power (Rom. 5:10)
His Advent and its Issues (1 Thess. 4:14, 15)

42 Christ for and in Us

On the Cross (2 Cor. 5:19)—Our Substitute
On the Throne (Heb. 9:24)—Our Representative
In the Heart (Eph. 3:17)—Our Strength

43 Ruin, Remedy, Result

Ruin in Adam (Eph. 2:3)—Fallen
Recovery in Christ (Eph. 2:5, 6)—Risen
Result in Me (Eph. 2:10)—Regenerated
> The *First* is what we inherit by Nature
> The *Second* is what we receive through Grace
> The *Third* is wrought in us by the Spirit

44 Casting Down, Lifting Up, Saving

An Old Time Gospel, in Job 22:29
Casting Down of the Sinner (Matt. 15:26-28)
Lifting Up of the Savior (John 3:14, 15)
Saving of the Believer (Acts 16:31)
> Conviction is by the Spirit of God
> Conversion is by Faith in Christ
> Confession is the result of both

45 Peace, in a Time of War

A Message of Mercy and Judgment from Deut. 20:10-12
Peace Proclaimed (v. 10, with Rom. 10:15)
Surrender Demanded (v. 11, with Acts 20:21)
Submission Secured (v. 11, with Acts 11:21)
Retribution Effected (v. 12, with 2 Thess. 1:7-9)

46   Mercy and Judgment

The Psalmist's Song (Ps. 100:1)
Mercy of God (Titus 3:5), in the Believer's Salvation
Judgment of God (Heb. 10:27), Unbeliever's Damnation

47   Ready

The Sinner is "ready to perish" (Deut. 26:3)
The Savior is "ready to save" (Isa. 38:20)
The Saved One is "ready to answer" (1 Peter 3:15)
The Servant is "ready to preach" (Rom. 1:15)

48   The Work of Christ

He Came Down (John 6:38) to obey, as Son
He Laid Down (John 10:15) His Life, as a Sacrifice
He Sat Down (Heb. 1:3) in Resurrection, as Priest
He will Put Down (1 Cor. 15:24) all rule, as King

Within these Four Great Facts is embraced the mediatorial work, of the Lord Jesus, for God and man

49   Grace Abounding

Justified by Grace (Rom. 3:24)—Our Deliverance
Standing in Grace (Rom. 5:2)—Our Position
Disciplined under Grace (Titus 2:12)—Our Training
Hoping through Grace (2 Thess. 2:16)—Our Prospect

50   Things That Are Sure

A Sure Foundation (2 Tim. 2:19)—To Build on
A Sure Hope (Heb. 6:19)—To Lay Hold on
A Sure Word (2 Peter 1:19)—To Guide us
A Sure Reward (Prov. 9:18)—Awaiting us

51   Bond Service

Bond Servants of Sin (John 8:34)—By Nature
Bond Servants of Satan (Acts 26:18)—By Conquest
Bond Servants of Christ (Rom. 1:1)—By Grace

52   Four Typical Men

A Man full of Demons (Mark 5:9)—Satan's Power
A Man full of Leprosy (Luke 5:10)—Sin's Corruption
A Man full of Faith (Acts 6:5)—Salvation, Testimony
A Man full of the Holy Spirit (Acts 11:24)—To Serve

53   Trust in the Lord

For Salvation (Eph. 1:2)
For Peace (Isa. 26:4)
For Guidance (Ps. 37:5)

54   Faith's Triumph

A Noble Confession (Isa. 12:2)
A Good Resolve (Job 13:15)
A Grand Assurance (Prov. 29:25)

55   Christ, the Life

He is the Source of Life (John 1:4)
He is the Giver of Life (John 17:2)
He is the Sustenance of Life (John 6:51)
He is the Object of Life (Phil. 1:21)

56   The Effects of the Word of God

To Receive the Word gives "Great Joy" (Acts 8:8, 14)
To Love the Word brings "Great Peace" (Ps. 119:165)
To Keep the Word assures "Great Reward" (Ps. 19:11)

57   God's Divine Message

The Gospel for the Sinner, to be Received (Rom. 1:16)
The Truth is for the Saint, to be Desired (1 Peter 2:1)
The Light is for Servants, to Follow (Ps. 119:105)

> The Gospel is for our Salvation (Eph. 1:13)
> The Truth is for our Sanctification (John 17:17)
> The Light is for our Edification (Ps. 43:3)

58   "Things Concerning Himself"
(Luke 24:27)

He gave Himself for our Sins (Gal. 1:4)

He presents Himself for our Peace (Luke 24:36)

He will come Himself for our Glory (1 Thess. 4:16)

59   Babel Maxims, in Use Today
(Genesis 11:1-3)

"Let us make *Brick*"—Counterfeit Christians

"Let us build a *City*"—Our Cause, our Religion

"Let us make us a *Name*"—Our Denomination

> Babel is built of brick, Jerusalem of hewn stone (Isa. 54:11)
> Worldlings' home is here, Christians look for theirs' (Heb. 11:10)
> Professors exalt their own Names, Christians bear Christ's

60   Three Representative Men

Adam, the Natural Man (Gen. 3)—Ruin

Abel, the Believing Man (Gen. 4)—Redemption

Enoch, the Translated Man (Gen. 5)—Glorification

> With Adam, connect Rom. 5:12
> With Abel, connect Heb. 11:4
> With Enoch, connect 1 Cor. 15:51

61   Four Personal Possessions

My Sins (Isa. 28:17)—A Weighty Burden

My Savior (Luke 1:47)—A Mighty Deliverer

My Salvation (Isa. 12:2)—A Joyful Possession

My Lord (Phil. 3)—A Personal Confession

62   John's Testimony to Jesus
(John 1:27-29)

The Lamb of God, v. 27—In Death

The Baptizer with the Spirit, v. 33—In Resurrection

The Son of God, v. 34—For Eternity

> Calvary is before Pentecost. Sin put away, the Spirit comes. The sinner is first saved, then sealed (v. 27). 1. A work done (v. 33). 2. A work being done (v. 34). 3. Is the One who is coming again (1 Thess. 1:9)

63   A Great Deliverance
(Psalm 116:1-2)

A Grand Declaration, v. 1—"I love the Lord"
A Great Deliverance, v. 2—"Because He heard"
A Good Determination, v. 2—"Therefore, will I call"

Connect with the *First* (1 John 4:19)
Link with the *Second* (Ps. 40:1-2)
Add to the *Third* (Ps. 40:3-4)

64   Grace and Glory
(Titus 2:11-13)

Grace has already Appeared—In the Cross of Christ
Glory will soon Appear—At the Lord's Coming
Godliness is now to Appear—In the Believer's Life

With the *First*, read John 1:14; Heb. 2:9
To the *Second*, link Col. 3:4; Jude 24
With the *Third*, connect 1 John 3:3; 1 Thess. 3:13

65   Great Transactions
In Colossians 1:12, 13

"Who Delivered" (v. 13)—A Great Deliverance
"Who Translated" (v. 13)—A Mighty Transition
"Who made Meet" (v. 12)—A Full Qualification

66   Old-fashioned Conversions
In 1 Thessalonians 1:9, 10

Past—"Ye turned to God from Idols"
Present—"To serve the Living and True God"
Future—"To wait for His Son"

The *First* is proof of true *Faith*
The *Second* is the result of real *Love*
The *Third* is the outlook of good *Hope*

67   The Savior's Invitations

Come—to the Thirsty, for Drink (John 7:37)
Come—to the Weary, for Rest (Matt. 11:28)
Come—to the Seeking, for Salvation (Luke 19:5)

The *Freeness* of the *First* is seen in Rev. 22:17
The *Fulness* of the *Second* is proved by Isa. 14:3
The *Guarantee* of the *Third* is given in John 6:37

68   God's Great Things

His Gift is Unspeakable (2 Cor. 9:15)
His Wisdom is Unsearchable (Rom. 11:33)
His Peace passeth Understanding (Phil. 4:7)
His Love is Unfathomable (Eph. 3:19)

69   Faith's Progress

(As Recorded in Psalm 37)

Trust in the Lord, v. 3—Salvation
Delight in the Lord, v. 4—Communion
Commit thy Way to the Lord, v. 5—Guidance
Rest in the Lord, v. 7—Patience
Wait on the Lord, v. 34—Hope

70   How the Gospel Is Treated

The Gospel Preached (1 Thess. 1:5)—In Power
The Gospel Pervertd (Gal. 1:7)—In Opposition
The Gospel Hid (2 Cor. 4:4)—For Condemnation
The Gospel Received (1 Cor. 15:1)—Unto Salvation

The Message, the power, the result, and the opposition, are the same now as ever. Wherever God's Gospel is preached in the Holy Spirit, sinners will be "arrested," some unto salvation, others to resist and oppose (Acts 2:37; 7:54)

71   The Gospel

The Gospel of God (Rom. 1:1)—Its Divine Author
The Gospel of Christ (Mark 1:1)—Its Grand Theme
The Gospel of Salvation (Eph. 1:18)—Its Great Object

Other Gospels are all Frauds
Other Names have no Value
Other Objects are all Worthless

72   Christ, the Rock

As a Foundation to Build on (1 Peter 2:4)
As a Cleft to Hide in (Song of Sol. 2:14)
As a Shadow to Shelter (Ps. 32:2)
As a Fortress to Defend (Ps. 31:3)

On Christ, *in* Christ, *under* Christ, and *within* Christ, express our faith in these presentations of Him

73   The Work of Christ

He Died as our Ransom (1 Tim. 2:6)—Deliverance
He Rose as our Justification (Rom. 4:25)—Liberty
He Lives as our Savior (Rom. 5:10)—Our Security
He Comes as our Glorifier (2 Thess. 1:10)—Our Goal

74   The Wrath of God

Predicted, for the Sinner (Job 36:18)
Endured, by the Savior (Ps. 88:7)
Escaped, by the Believer (1 Thess. 1:10)
Abideth, on the Unbeliever (John 3:36)

This solemn and much disputed truth, was often spoken of by the Lord, much by His apostles, and needs to be plainly, scripturally, and feelingly testified of by all who preach Christ, who is Judge as well as Savior.

75 The Believing Soul and the Savior

Comes to Christ for Salvation (John 6:37)
Enters into Christ for Security (John 10:9)
Builds on Christ for Stability (1 Peter 2:6)
Eats of Christ for Strength (John 6:57)

> "Christ is All, from first to last,
> The same today as in the past"

76 Christ's Work for Us

Finished on the Cross (John 19:31)
Accepted in the Resurrection (Rom. 4:25)
Manifested on the Throne (Heb. 1:3)

> The rent veil, the opened graves, the filled throne, are the witnesses to the perfection, acceptance, and sufficiency thereof

77 God's Work in Us

Commenced at Regeneration (Phil. 1:6)
Continued throughout Life (Phil. 2:12, 13)
Completed at Glorification (Phil. 3:21)

78 The Lord "Knocking" at the Door

Of the Sinner (Rev. 3:20)—With Salvation
Of the Saint (Song of Sol. 5:2)—For Communion
Of the Servant (Luke 12:26)—For Reward

> Reception of Christ to the heart is necessary to communion, and communion is the right condition for effective and acceptable service

79 Grace and Works

Salvation is by Grace, not of Works (Eph. 2:8, 9)
The Saved are Created to Good Works (Eph. 2:10)
Not by Works, but in Mercy God Saves (Titus 3:5)
Believers are to Maintain Good Works (Titus 3:8)

> *Legalists* put works in a wrong place (Gal. 5:4)
> *Professors* give them no place at all (Titus 1:16)
> *Christians* are zealous of good works (Titus 2:14)

80 Fountain, Well, and Streams

Illustrative of Divine Life and Healing
(Song of Solomon 4:15)

The Fountain, God the Great Giver (Rev. 22:6)
The Well, Christ in Whom it is Stored (Col. 3:3)
Streams, the Spirit, by Whom it comes (1 Thess. 1:5)

Taking it, is the Sinner's Responsibility (Rev. 22:17)
Possessing it, is the Believer's Privilege (John 4:14)
Distributing it, is the Christian's Service (John 7:38)

81 Noble Bereans

(Acts 17:10-13)

The Word Preached by Paul—in Faithfulness
The Word Readily Received—in Confidence
The Word Daily Searched—for Confirmation

A wise preacher, willing hearers, honest inquirers, produce true believers.

82 Gracious Invitations

To the Weary (Matt. 11:28)—Come and Rest
To the Thirsty (Isa. 55:1)—Come and Drink
To the Hungry (Luke 14:17)—Come and Eat

83 Raiment

Human Rags of Selfrighteousness (Isa. 64:5)
Garments Patched by Reformation (Mark 2:21)
The Best Robe bestowed in Grace (Luke 15:22)
Divine Righteousness received by Faith (Rom. 3:22)

1. These have to be Stripped Off
2. This has to be Cast Away
3. Provided by God, and made known in the Gospel
4. Accepted, Confessed, and Manifested

84 The All-powerful Word

The Word Received (2 Thess. 1:6)—in Faith
The Word Obeyed (1 Thess. 2:13)—in Practice
The Word Sounded Forth (1 Thess. 1:8)—in Testimony
  1. The Message of Reconciliation
  2. The Means of Sanctification
  3. The Mission of Evangelization

85 Tenses of Christian Life

Such *were* some of You (1 Cor. 6:2)
Now *are* we Sons of God (1 John 3:2)
We *shall be* like Him (1 John 3:2)
  1. By Nature and in Practice
  2. By Regeneration and Manifestation
  3. By Transformation and Glorification

86 Three Views of Christ

We beheld Him (Luke 23:35)—Dying
We behold Him (2 Cor. 3:18)—Living
We shall see Him (Rev. 5:6)—Reigning
  1. Faith's View of the Cross, in Salvation
  2. Love's Gaze to the Throne, for Transformation
  3. Hope's Outlook in the Future, for Association

87 Cardinal Truths

Justification, by Blood—A New Standing
Regeneration, by the Spirit—A New Life
Sanctification, through the Word—A New Walk
Glorification, at Christ's Coming—A New Condition
  Rom. 5:9; John 3:5; John 17:17; 2 Thess. 1:10

88 The Power of God's Word
In the Sinner's Conviction and Conversion

As a Mirror, it shows man's Condition (James 1:23-24)
As a Hammer, it breaks down his Pride (Jer. 23:29)
As a Sword, it pierces his Conscience (Hcb. 4:12)
As Balm, it brings healing to his Soul (Ps. 107:20)

89   Christ's All sufficiency

No other Name (Acts 4:12)—for Salvation
No other Righteousness (Phil. 3:9)—for Acceptance
No other Lord (1 Cor. 8:6)—for Submission

90   Spiritual Life

Its Reception, Maintainance, and Manifestation

Received by Faith, at New Birth (John 20:31)
Sustained by Feeding on Christ (John 6:57)
Strengthened by the Indwelling Spirit (Eph. 3:16)
Manifested in the Believer's Body (2 Cor. 4:11)

91   Past, Present, Future

What I was by Nature (Eph. 2:3)
What I did in Practice (Titus 3:3)
What I am by Grace (Eph. 2:8, 10)
What I shall be in Glory (1 John 3:2)

92   Stages in Man's Life

His Condition (Isa. 59:2)—Severed from God
His Character (Rom. 8:7)—At Enmity with God
His Conversion (Col. 1:21)—Reconciled to God
His Conduct (1 Thess. 2:12)—Walking worthy of God

93   Boundless and Free

God's Love is to the Unlovely (1 John 4:10)
Christ's Death is for the Ungodly (Rom. 5:6)
Salvation is for the Undeserving (Acts 28:28)
     1. No call for any Virtue
     2. No need for any Reform
     3. No place for any Claim

94   The Savior

A Savior Provided by God (1 John 4:12)
A Savior Presented in the Gospel (2 Tim. 1:10)
A Savior Possessed by Faith (1 Tim. 4:10)
> Provided for All, Presented to All, but not Possessed by All

95   Necessities

We must needs Die (2 Sam. 14:14)
Christ must needs Suffer (Acts 17:3)
The Scripture must needs be Fulfilled (Acts 1:16)
> 1. The Wages and Result of Sin
> 2. The Only Way of Atonement and Reconciliation
> 3. Alike in Salvation and in Judgment

96   Sin and Its Results

Its Origin in Eden (Rom. 5:12)
Its Practice by All (Rom. 3:23)
Its Results Now (John 8:36)
Its Judgment Hereafter (James 1:15)

97   What Christ Has Done for Our Sins

Christ died for our Sins (1 Cor. 15:3)
Christ gave Himself for our Sins (Gal. 1:4)
Christ bare our Sins (1 Peter 2:24)
Christ loosed us from our Sins (Rev. 1:5)

98   True Worshipers
(John 4:23)

The Leper who was Cleansed (Luke 17:15)
The Blind Man who was Healed (John 9:38)
The Disciples who Followed (Matt. 28:17)
The Redeemed in Glory (Rev. 5:11)

99   Personal Acceptance of Christ

He loved Me (Gal. 2:20)
He gave Himself for Me (Gal. 2:20)
He is My Savior (Luke 1:47)
He is My Lord (John 20:28)

100   The Love of God

It is an Everlasting Love (Jer. 31:3)
It is a Manifested Love (1 John 4:9)
It is a Redeeming Love (Isa. 63:9)
It is a Persevering Love (Rom. 8:39)

101   Man in Nature

A Child of Wrath (Eph. 2:3)—By Birth
A Stranger to Christ (Eph. 2:12)—In Heart
An Enemy of God (Rom. 5:10)—In Mind
A Wanderer from God (Isa. 53:6)—In Way
An Object of God's Love (Rom. 5:8)—For Salvation

102   The Lamb As a Sacrifice

A Lamb Demanded (Gen. 22:7)
A Lamb Provided (Gen. 22:8)
The Lamb Manifested (John 1:29)
The Lamb Sacrificed (1 Peter 1:9)
The Lamb Glorified (Rev. 5:6)

103   The Son of God

His Own Son (Rom. 8:32)
His Only Begotten Son (John 3:16)
His Beloved Son (Matt. 3:17)
His Dear Son (Col. 1:13)
His Crucified Son (Matt. 27:54)
His Glorified Son (Acts 3:13)

104   God's Command and Call
(Acts 18:30)

A Great Command—"God Commandeth"
A Universal Call—"All Men"
A World Wide Sphere—"Everywhere"
A Definite Object—"To Repent"
A Specified Time—"Now"

105   The World

In Degradation (1 John 5:19)—Its Ruin
In Condemnation (Rom. 3:19)—Its Guilt
Its Propitiation (1 John 2:2)—God's Remedy
Its Evangelization (Mark 16:15)—Its Opportunity

106   Looking to Christ

As the Uplifted Savior (Isa. 45:22; John 3:14)
As the Glorified Examplar (Heb. 12:2)
As the Coming Deliverer (Phil. 3:21)

107   The Marks of Regeneration

A Nature which is from God (2 Peter 1:4)
An Image which is of God (Col. 3:10)
A Holiness which is for God (1 John 3:9)
A Love which is like God (1 John 5:2)

108   The Gospel Call

It is by God's Grace (Gal. 1:15)
It is of His Son (Rom. 1:6)
It is through the Gospel (2 Thess. 2:4)
It is in the Spirit (1 Cor. 1:24; 2:4)

109   Nothing

"Nothing but Leaves" (Matt. 22:29)—Man's Religion
"Nothing Bettered" (Mark 5:26)—Man's Reformation
"Nothing to Pay" (Luke 7:42)—Man's Bankruptcy
"Nothing Amiss" (Luke 23:31)—Christ's Perfection

110 "The Man Christ Jesus"

A Man approved of God (Acts 2:22)—In Life
A Man of Sorrows (Isa. 53:3)—In Death
A Man Glorified (Acts 7:51)—In Heaven

111 The Lamb

Blood of the Lamb—Our Title to Heaven
Worship of the Lamb—Employment of Redeemed
Marriage of the Lamb—Glory of the Church
Wrath of the Lamb—Doom of the Lost
Rev. 7:14; Rev. 5:8, 12; Rev. 19:7; Rev. 6:16

112 The Mighty Power of God

In Salvation of Sinners (Rom. 1:16)
In Preservation of the Saved (1 Peter 1:5)
In Strengthening for Conflict (Eph. 6:10)
In Efficiency for Service (2 Cor. 6:7)

113 The Grace of God

Brings Salvation to All (Titus 2:10)
Justifies all Believers (Rom. 3:24)
Abounds toward all Saints (2 Cor. 9:9)

114 Repentance, False and True

Pharoah, hardened in Sin (Exod. 10:16)
Balaam, held by Covetousness (Num. 22:14)
Judas, possessed by Satan (Matt. 27:4)
The Prodigal, convicted and returning (Luke 15:18)

115 The Blood of Christ

Offered to God in Atonement (Heb. 9:14)
Justifies the Soul from Guilt (Rom. 5:9)
Looses from Sin's Power (Rev. 1:5)
Cleanses from Sin's Defilement (1 John 1:7)

116 Marks of Genuine Conversion

Repentance toward God (Acts 20:31)
Returning to God (Ps. 119:59)
Receiving the Word of God (Acts 2:41)
Rejoicing in God (Rom. 5:11)

117 The Coming of Christ

As the Dayspring, at His Birth (Luke 1:78)
As the Daysman, in His Death (John 9:33)
As the Day Star, at His Advent (2 Peter 1:19)
  1. He brought Light and Life by His Incarnation (John 1:4)
  2. He made Reconciliation and Peace in His Death (Rom. 5:10; Col. 1:20)
  3. He will bring Immortality and Victory at His Coming (1 Cor. 15:52, 56)

118 New Things

A New Covenant by Redemption (Heb. 12:24)
A New Creation in Regeneration (Gal. 6:15)
A New Song in Resurrection Life (Ps. 40:3)
A New Walk in Righteousness (Ps. 23:3)

119 Christ Is Able

To Save to the Uttermost (Heb. 7:25)
To Succor to the Fullest (Heb. 2:18)
To Subdue to the Last (Phil. 3:21)
  He Saves by His Death
  He Succors by His Risen Life
  He Subdues by His Kingly Power

120 The Soul

The Sin of the Soul (Ezek. 18:20)—Our Guilt
The Sacrifice of the Soul (Isa. 53:10)—Christ's Work
The Salvation of the Soul (1 Peter 1:9)—God's Power
The Soul's Satisfaction (Ps. 63:5)—Christ's Person

121   Midnight Scenes

A Midnight of Judgment (Exod. 12:12, 29)
A Midnight of Salvation (Acts 16:25-31)
A Midnight of Praise (Ps. 119:62)
A Midnight of Separation (Matt. 25:6)
1. On the Ungodly World
2. To the Awakened Sinner
3. Of the Converted Soul
4. Of the Saved and Unsaved

122   Love and Its Object

Its Source (1 John 4:7)—"Love is of God"
Its Exhibition (1 John 4:8)—In sending "His Son"
Its Object (1 John 4:9)—"That we might Live"

123   The Word of God

Is Penetrating (Heb. 4:12)—It Pierces
Is Healthgiving (Ps. 107:20)—It Heals
Is Powerful (Jer. 23:29)—It Breaks
Is Quickening (1 Peter 1:23)—It Regenerates
Is Separating (Ps. 119:8, 9)—It Cleanses

124 Christ's Comings and Their Purpose

He came to do God's Will (Heb. 10:9)
He came to Save Sinners (1 Tim. 1:15)
He will come to Gather Saints (Heb. 10:28)
He will come to Judge the Nations (Rev. 1:7)

125   Spiritual Uplifts

The Face Uplifted to God (Job 22:26)
The Voice Uplifted in Praise (Isa. 24:14)
The Hands Uplifted in Prayer (Ps. 6:3, 4)
The Head Uplifted in Hope (Luke 21:28)
1. The Sinner's Reconciliation and Conversion
2. The Saved One's Song of Thanksgiving
3. The Suppliant in the Place of Dependence
4. The Sufferer looking for the Deliverer

126   From the Cross to the Throne

"Lifted up" as a Sacrifice (John 3:14, 15)
"Raised up" as a Savior (2 Cor. 4:14)
"Received up" as a Victor (Mark 16:19)

127   Three Bible Mountains

Mount of Sacrifice (Gen. 22:1-14)—Redemption
Mount of Instruction (Matt. 5:1)—Discipleship
Mount of Transfiguration (Matt. 17:1)—Glory

128   Trees and Their Message

A Corrupt Tree (Matt. 7:17)—Sin in the Nature
A Barren Tree (Matt. 21:19)—Empty Profession
A Planted Tree (Matt. 15:13)—True Conversion
A Fruitful Tree (Ps. 1:3)—Abiding in Grace

129   Redemption

Obtained at the Cross (Heb. 9:12)
Made Known in the Gospel (Ps. 111:9)
Experienced by the Believer (Eph. 1:7)

130   Peace

Made at Christ's Death (Col. 1:20)
Manifested in Resurrection (John 20:19, 20)
Mine in Believing (Rom. 5:1)

131   Gospel Blessings

Saved according to His Mercy (Titus 3:5)
Forgiven according to His Grace (Eph. 1:7)
Strengthened according to His Power (Col. 1:11)

132 What Christ Does for All Believers

He Died to Redeem (Titus 2:14)
He Rose to Justify (Rom. 4:25)
He Lives to Save (Heb. 7:25)
He Comes to Glorify (2 Thess. 1:10)

133   **Three Vital Facts**

Recorded in Hebrews 9:27-28

Sentence on Sin Pronounced (v. 27)
Sacrifice for Sin Accepted (v. 28)
Salvation from Sin Completed (v. 28)

134   **The Sinner's Position**

"Afar off," as Aliens (Eph. 2:12, 13)—In Nature
"Afar off," as Unclean (Luke 17:14)—In Life
"Afar off," after Death (Luke 16:23)—In Hell

135   **The Salvation of God**

God has Sent It (Acts 28:28)
Grace has Brought It (Titus 2:11)
The Gospel Proclaims It (Eph. 1:13)
Faith Receives It (Rom. 1:16)

136   **The Forgiveness of Sins**

Has been Procured by the Cross (Eph. 1:7)
Is Made Known in the Gospel (Acts 26:18)
Is Received through Believing (Acts 10:43)
Is Assured by the Word (1 John 2:12)

137   **Three Great Questions**

Who then can be Saved? (Mark 10:26)
What must I do to be Saved? (Acts 16:30)
How shall we escape if we Neglect? (Heb. 2:3)

Answers—1. If *any* Man enter in (John 10:9)
2. Believe on the Lord Jesus Christ (Acts 16:31)
3. They shall not escape (Heb. 12:25)

138   **Happy Days**

The Happy Day of Conversion (Acts 8:39)
Happy Days of Service (1 Kings 10:8)
Happy Lives in Obedience (John 13:17)
Happy when we see the Lord (John 16:22)

139   The Heavenly Race and Reward

A Good Start (Acts 9:20)—Conversion
A Clean Stripping (Heb. 12:1)—Separation
A Straight Course (Phil. 3:14)—Devotion
A Good Ending (2 Tim. 4:7, 8)—Glorification

140   Threefold View of Christ

On the Cross (John 19:17-19)—The Dying Surety
On the Throne (Heb. 10:12)—A Living Representative
In the Heart (Eph. 3:17)—Our Indwelling Strength

> As Sinners, we begin with Christ Dying
> As Saved, we need Christ Living
> As Saints, we have Christ Indwelling

141   Spiritual Life

Regeneration (Titus 3:5)—Life Originated
Renewal (2 Cor. 4:16)—Life Sustained
Resurrection (1 Cor. 15:22)—Life Victorious

> The New Birth is a definite Act (John 1:12, 13)
> Growth is a Gradual Process (1 Peter 2:2)
> Glorification is a grand Consummation (Phil. 3:20)

142   Three Impossibilities

Cannot serve God and Mammon (Matt. 6:24)
Cannot partake with Christ and demons (1 Cor. 10:21)
Cannot live to self and Christ (Luke 14:26)

> There must be a Choice and Decision
> There will be Communion and Separation
> There can be Discipleship and Devotion

143   The Blood of the Lamb
(Exodus 12; 1 Peter 1:18, 19; Hebrews 11:28)

Blood Shed (v. 6; 1 Peter 1:19)—Atonement
Blood Preserved (v. 22; Rom. 3:25)—Propitiation
Blood Sprinkled by man (v. 7)—Appropriation
Blood Seen by Jehovah (v. 13)—Satisfaction

144   From Guilt to Grace

(Isaiah 6:1-8)

Conviction of State (v. 4; Job 42:5, 6)
Confession of Sin (v. 5; Ps. 51:4, 5)
Cleansing by Sacrifice (v. 7; Heb. 10:17-22)
Called to Service (v. 8; Heb. 9:14; 1 Thess. 1:9)

     1. The Work of the Spirit Within
     2. The Result manifested Without
     3. The Cross appropriated by Faith
     4. The Claims of God Owned

145   Filthy Garments to a Fair Crown

(Zechariah 3:1-8)

Stripped (v. 4, with Isa. 64:6; Job 27:6)
Cleansed (v. 4, with Heb. 1:3; Rev. 1:5)
Clothed (v. 5, with Luke 15:22; Phil. 3:9)
Crowned (v. 5, with Ps. 103:4; 1 Peter 2:9)

     1. The Sinner stripped of Self Righteousness
     2. The Soul cleansed by Christ's Blood
     3. The Saved clad in God's Righteousness
     4. The Saint crowned as a Royal Priest

146   God's Revelations

God's Wrath revealed (Rom. 1:18)—In Judgment
God's Righteousness revealed (Rom. 1:17)—In Gospel
Christ's Person revealed (Gal. 1:16)—To the Soul
Glory to be revealed (Rom. 8:18)—At His Coming

147   God's Fixed Conditions

Without Shed Blood (Heb. 9:22)—No Remission
Without Faith (Heb. 5:38; 11:6)—No Salvation
Without Holiness (Heb. 12:14)—No Heaven

     The Unitarian denies Christ's Atonement
     The Rationalist rejects God's Revelation
     The Antinomiam refuses Heaven's Holiness

148   Persuading

Persuading Men (2 Cor. 5:11)—The Preacher's Work
Almost Persuaded (Acts 26:28)—The Procrastinator
Never Persuaded (Luke 16:31)—The Unbeliever
Fully Persuaded (Rom. 8:38, 39)—The Christian

149   God's Resources for Sinners

Abundant Mercy (1 Peter 1:3)—For the Lost
Abundant Grace (1 Tim. 1:14)—For the Needy
Abundant Pardon (Isa. 55:7)—For the Guilty
> In our Misery, we need Mercy
> In our Worthlessness, we need Grace
> In our Criminality, we need Clemency

150   Three Impossibilities

The Natural man cannot please God (Rom. 8:6)
A Bad Nature cannot yield good Fruit (Matt. 7:18)
The Unregenerate cannot see the Kingdom (John 3:3)
> The Bankruptcy of Adam's Race
> The Corruption of Man's Being
> The Incapacity of Fallen Humanity

151 A Great Question and Its Answer

"How shall I put thee among the Children?" (Jer. 3:19)
> Answers—1. By Receiving God's Son (John 1:12)
>   2. By Birth of God's Spirit (1 John 5:1)
>   3. By Call of God's Grace (1 John 3:1)

152   Three of God's "Comes"

A Summons to the Careless (Isa. 1:18)
An Invitation to the Weary (Matt. 11:28)
A Call to the Thirsty (John 7:37)

153   Mighty Acts of the Lord:
Wrought for all that Believe

Redemption from Sin's Slavery (Titus 2:14)
Resurrection from Sin's Death (Eph. 2:1)
Release from Sin's Practice (Rev. 1:5)
1. By Christ's Death on the Cross
2. By Christ's Life in Heaven
3. In Christ's Blood Applied

154   "My Salvation"
(Isaiah 12:2)

It is "*by* Christ Jesus" (1 Thess. 5:9)
It is "*in* Christ Jesus" (2 Tim. 2:10)
1. He is its Author and Cause (Heb. 2:10)
2. In Him is its Security (Rom. 5:9)

155   The Grace of God

It *Justifies* the Guilty (Rom. 3:24)
It *Saves* the Lost (Eph. 2:8)
It *Reigns* for the World (Rom. 5:21)
It *Abounds* to the Church (2 Cor. 9:8)

156   Christ Is Able

To *Save* to the Uttermost (Heb. 7:25)
To *Succor* in Temptation(Heb. 2:18)
To *Keep* from Stumbling (Jude 24)
To *Subdue* all Things (Phil. 3:21)
1. By His Blood and Power
2. By His Priesthood in Heaven
3. As our Shepherd and Advocate
4. As our Lord and King

157   Blood-bought Blessings
Possessed by all Believers

A *Forgiveness* which it Bought (Col. 1:14)
A *Peace* which it Made (Col. 1:20)
A *Nearness* which it Gives (Eph. 2:13)
A *Cleansing* which it Effects (1 John 1:7)

158   Three Great "I Wills" of Christ

I will Give you Rest (Matt. 11:28)
I will in No Wise Cast Out (John 6:37)
I will Receive you to Myself (John 14:3)

His Promise to the Sinner Coming
His Assurance to the Soul Trusting
His Announcement to the Saint Waiting

159   Son, Surety, Sacrifice

As Son, He is well pleasing to God (Matt. 3:17)
As Surety, He gave satisfaction to God (Heb. 7:22)
As Sacrifice, His work is accepted by God (Eph. 5:2)

1. His Person gives Value to His Work
2. His Atonement meets all Divine Claims
3. His Work gives Acceptance to His People

160   Pardon, Peace, and Power

Pardon Proclaimed in Christ's Name (Acts 13:38)
Peace Imparted by Christ's Word (John 20:19-21)
Power Bestowed by Christ's Gift (Acts 1:8)

161   Drink for the Thirsty

Broken Cisterns (Jer. 2:13)
Thirsty Souls (Isa. 55:1)
A Living Fountain (Rev. 21:6)
A Royal Invitation (Rev. 22:17)

162 Conviction, Contrition, Cleansing
(Psalm 51)

Conviction of Sin, by the Word (v. 4)
Contrition for Sin, on the Lip (v. 5)
Cleansing from Sin, by the Blood (v. 7)

1. Conviction comes when the Sinner sees God (Job 42:5, 6)
2. Confession then is made unto God (Ps. 32:5)
3. Conversion results from Cleansing by God (Luke 17:15)

163 Hearts

A *Deceitful* Heart, by Nature (Jer. 17:9)
A *Double* Heart, in Hypocrisy (Ps. 12:2)
A *Deceived* Heart, through Ignorance (Isa. 44:20)
A *Hardened* Heart, through Unbelief (Mark 8:17)

164 Hearts

An *Honest* Heart receives God's Word
An *Opened* Heart yields to God's Hand
A *Believing* Heart welcomes God's Righteousness
A *Glad* Heart rejoices in His Salvation

Luke 8:15; Acts 16:14; Rom. 10:9; Ps. 4:7

165 Three Night Scenes

A Night at Philippi (Acts 16:25)—Awakening
A Night in Jerusalem (John 3:1)—Anxiety
A Night on the Adriatic (Acts 27:23)—Assurance

The Three Stages illustrate the Soul's Progress from Sin to Salvation

166 Three Seals

The Savior Sealed for Sacrifice (John 6:27)
The Believer Sealed for Glory (Eph. 1:13)
The Sinner Sealed for Judgment (Job 14:17)

167   Only a Sparrow
Emblematic of a Sinner in Nature and Grace
Of little Value to Men (Matt. 8:29)
Cared for and Watched by God (Luke 12:6)
Redeemed and Freed by Substitution (Lev. 14:4, 6)
Nesting in God's Temple (Ps. 84:3)

168   Emblems of Man
In Nature and in Grace
A Black Ethiopian (Jer. 13:23)—Cannot be Cleansed
A Wild Colt (Job 11:23)—Cannot be Trained
A Spotted Leopard (Jer 13:23)—Cannot Change
A Rescued Sheep (Luke 15:4, 6)—Cannot be Lost

169   Three Bible "Doors"
An Open Door of Salvation (Acts 14:27)
A Closed Door of Neglect (Rev. 3:20)
A Shut Door for Judgment (Luke 13:25)
    1. Opened by God to admit the Sinner
    2. Opened by the Sinner to let in the Savior
    3. Closed by Christ to exclude the Despiser

170   Three Great "Whosoevers"
A *Whosoever* of Forgiveness (Acts 10:43)
A *Whosoever* of Salvation (John 3:16)
A *Whosoever* of Condemnation (Rev. 20:15)
    1. A Proclamation unto All
    2. An Assurance for All
    3. A Warning to All

171   Three Conditions

What I *Was* (Eph. 2:3)—A Child of Wrath
What I *Am* (1 John 3:1)—A Son of God
What I *Shall* Be (Rom. 8:17)—Joint Heir with Christ

172   Eternal Life

Eternal Life in Promise (Titus 1:1; John 10:10)
Eternal Life in Possession (John 10:28; 1 John 5:13)
Eternal Life in Prospect (Rom. 5:21)

    1. Before the Cross of Christ (John 1:4)
    2. Now Received in Believing (John 20:31)
    3. Awaiting its Final Triumph (2 Cor. 5:4)

173   Our Salvation

Procured by Christ's Death (1 Cor. 15:2, 3)
Possessed by Faith in Christ (Acts 16:31)
Assured by God's Word (1 John 5:1)
Insured by Christ's Life (Rom. 5:9)
Perfected at Christ's Return (Heb. 9:28)

174   The New Birth

The Worker (John 3:5)—The Spirit of God
The Instrument (1 Peter 1:23)—The Word of God
The Subject (1 John 5:1)—The Believing Sinner
The Result (Gal. 3:26)—a Child of God

175   Biography of Nicodemus

He Came to Christ (John 3:1)
He Spoke for Christ (John 7:50, 51)
He Honored Christ (John 19:39)

    Coming to Him for Salvation
    Speaking of Him in Confession
    Honoring Him in Service

176   Eternal Realities

Eternal Redemption (Heb. 9:12)
Eternal Salvation (Heb. 5:9)
Eternal Life (1 John 5:11)
Eternal Glory (1 Peter 5:10)
Eternal Fire (Jude 7)
    1. Wrought by Christ
    2. Proclaimed in the Gospel
    3. Possessed by Believers
    4. In Prospect for the Saved
    5. Awaiting Christ-rejecters

177   Pictures of the Unconverted

Bondslaves of Sin (John 8:34)
Children of Disobedience (Col. 3:6)
Sheep going Astray (Isa. 53:6)
Enemies in Practice (Col. 1:21)

178   Pictures of the Converted

Freemen of Christ (John 8:36)
Obedient Children of God (1 Peter 1:14)
Sheep Returned to the Shepherd (1 Peter 2:25)
Friends in Communion (John 15:15)

179   Scripture Cups

Christ's Cup of Suffering (Matt. 26:39)
God's Cup of Salvation (Ps. 116:13)
Believer's Cup of Blessing (Ps. 23:5)
Sinner's Cup of Retribution (Ps. 11:6)

180   The Call of God
Through the Gospel

Out of Sin unto Repentance (Matt. 9:13)
Out of Darkness into Light (1 Peter 2:9)
Out of Corruption unto Holiness (1 Thess. 4:7)
    1. The State—Salvation
    2. The Sphere—Communion
    3. The Condition—Separation

181   Life's Turnings

Turned to his own Way (Isa. 53:6)
Turned unto the Lord (Acts 11:21)
Turned to the Word (Ps. 119:59)
Turned into Hell (Ps. 9:17)

1. The Sinner's Pathway
2. The Result of Faith
3. The Christian's Counsellor
4. The Christ-rejecter's Doom

182   Three Grand Gospel Facts

The Blood of Christ shed *for* us (Matt. 26:28)
The Holy Ghost shed *on* us (Titus 3:6)
The Love of God shed abroad *in* us (Rom. 5:5)

1. To Procure our Salvation
2. To Provide our Strength
3. To Preserve our Spirituality

183   The Name of Jesus

There is Salvation in it (Acts 4:12)
There is Remission by it (Acts 10:43)
There is Life through it (John 20:31)

184   What Christ Was Made for Us

He was made Flesh (John 1:14)—Incarnation
He was of no Reputation (Phil. 2:7)—Humiliation
He was made Sin (2 Cor. 5:21)—Substitution
He was made a Curse (Gal. 3:13)—Satisfaction

185 What Christ Is Now Made by God

He is made Lord and Christ (Acts 2:36)
He is made Better than Angels (Heb. 1:4)
He is made Head of the Corner (1 Peter 2:7)
He is made a High Priest (Heb. 5:5)

186   What Christ Is Made to Us
To all who Believe, He is
Made Wisdom (1 Cor. 1:30; Col. 2:3)
Made Righteousness (1 Cor. 1:30; 2 Cor. 5:21)
Made Sanctification (1 Cor. 1:30; Heb. 2:11)
Made Redemption (1 Cor. 1:30; Eph. 4:30)

187   The Heart of Man
Deceitful above all things (Jer. 17:9)—By Nature
Opened to receive the Word (Acts 16:14)—By Grace
Believing unto Righteousness (Rom. 10:10)—In Faith
Cleaving unto the Lord (Acts 11:23)—In Purpose
Hardened in Rejecting Christ (Heb. 3:15)—By Sin

188   Trusting in the Lord
Trusting in Him for Salvation (Prov. 29:25)
Trusting in Him for Peace (Isa. 26:3)
Trusting in Him for Preservation (Ps. 61:4)

189   Cleansing
By Blood from Sin's Guilt (1 John 1:7)
By the Word from Sin's Defilement (Eph. 5:26)
By Separation from Sin's Practice (2 Cor. 7:1)

190   The Atoning Death of Christ
Its Necessity (Heb. 9:22)
Its Efficacy (Heb. 1:3)
Its Permanency (Heb. 10:12)
Its Power (Heb. 10:19-22)

191   Peace With God
Its Solid Basis (Eph. 2:14)—Christ Himself
Its Procuring Cause (Col. 1:20)—His Perfect Work
Its Glorious Message (Rom. 10:15)—In the Gospel
Its Sure Possession (Rom. 5:1)—By Faith

192   Attitudes of the Soul

Running from God (Isa. 53:6)
Repentance toward God (Acts 20:21)
Reconciliation with God (Rom. 5:10)

193   A Gospel to All

Gospel of Grace (Acts 20:24
Gospel of Peace (Rom. 10:15)
Gospel of Salvation (Eph. 1:13)
> 1. God's Declaration to the *Guilty*
> 2. God's Message to the *Troubled*
> 3. God's Good News to the *Lost*

194   Christ Is All

A Gift to be Received (John 1:12)
An Owner to be Confessed (Rom. 10:9)
A Teacher to be Heard (Luke 10:26)
A Shepherd to be Followed (John 10:27)
> Received by Faith as Savior
> Confessed by Lip as Lord
> Heard and Obeyed as Master
> Owned and Followed as Guide

195   The Lamb

The Lamb beheld as Sacrifice (John 1:29)
The Lamb looked on as Example (John 1:36)
The Lamb worshiped and Exalted (Rev. 5:5-10)
> A Look at Christ Crucified, *Saves*
> A Gaze on Christ Walking, *Attracts*
> A Sight of Christ Glorified, *Humbles*

196   Three Conditions

My State in Nature (Eph. 2:12)—Without Christ
My Standing by Grace (Eph. 1:1)—In Christ
My Place in Glory (Phil. 1:23)—With Christ

197   Three Stages of Experience

Turn from their Sin (1 Kings 8:35)—Repentance
Turn to the Lord (Lam. 3:40)—Reconciliation
Turn from your Idols (Ezek. 14:6)—Renunciation

> Repentance is wrought through the Word believed
> Reconciliation is brought in the Blood trusted
> Renunciation is easy when Christ is known

198   Christ's Great Gifts

He gave *Himself* a Sacrifice to God (Eph. 5:2)
He gave His *Life* a Ranson for us (Matt. 21)
He gives *Peace* as a Legacy to us (John 14:27)
He gives *Glory* as a Crown awaiting us (John 17:22)

199   Now

NOW, God commands Repentance (Acts 17:30)
NOW, is the Day of Salvation (2 Cor. 6:2)
NOW, there is full Justification (Rom. 5:9)
NOW, is there no Condemnation (Rom. 8:1)

> 1. God's Call to the Careless
> 2. God's Word to the Anxious
> 3. God's Declaration to the Believer
> 4. God's Assurance to the Christian

200   "I Will's" of Salvation

"I will Arise" (Luke 15:18)—Repentance
"I will Trust" (Isa. 12:2)—Conversion
"I will Offer" (Ps. 116:17)—Thanksgiving
"I will Run" (Ps. 119:32)—Discipleship

> 1. The Resolution of the Convicted Soul
> 2. The Confession of the Trusting One
> 3. The Desire of the Saved Sinner
> 4. The Decision of the Ardent Saint

201   Things Everlasting

"Everlasting Love" (Jer. 31:3)—God's Attitude
"Everlasting Life" (John 6:40)—God's Gift
"Everlasting Strength" (Isa. 26:4)— God's Power

202   Peace

No Peace (Isa. 57:21), to the Ungodly
False Peace (Jer. 8:11), deceives the Hypocrite
True Peace (Rom. 5:1), is given to the Believer
Perfect Peace (Isa. 26:3), is enjoyed by the Truster

203   A Fourfold View of Christ

A Sacrifice of Sin (1 Peter 3:18)
A Savior of Sinners (1 Tim. 1:15)
A Succorer of Saints (Heb. 2:18)
A Sender of Servants (Mark 16:15)

204   Beholds

"Behold the Man" (John 19:5)—Incarnate
"Behold the Lamb" (John 1:29)—Sacrificed
"Behold thy King" (John 12:15)—Exalted
"Behold He Cometh" (Rev. 1:7)—Unexpected

    1. The Person of Christ gives value to His work
    2. The Work of Christ procures our Salvation
    3. The Rule of Christ brings Blessing
    4. The Coming of Christ will bring judgment

205   Looks

The Love-look of God (Ezek. 16:8)
The Life-look of Sinners (Isa. 45:22
The Hope-look of Saints (Phil. 3:20)

    1. The Love of God is toward Sinners (Rom. 5:8)
    2. The Faith of the Soul is in Christ (Eph. 1:12)
    3. The Hope of Christians is on Christ (1 John 3:3)

206 The Eternal Trinity

The Eternal God is our Savior (Deut. 33:27)
The Eternal Son is our Redeemer (John 1:1)
The Eternal Spirit is our Sanctifier (Heb. 9:16)

207 Eternal Blessings

Eternal Life is God's Free Gift (Rom. 6:23)
Eternal Redemption, Christ's Purchase (Heb. 9:12)
Eternal Salvation, the Believer's Possession (Heb. 5:9)
Eternal Glory is the Believer's Prospect (1 Peter 5:10)

208 Sin

"The Pleasures of Sin" (Heb. 11:25)—Allure
"The Deceitfulness of Sin" (Heb. 3:13)—Deludes
"The Wages of Sin" (Rom. 6:23)—Sinner's Death
"A Sacrifice for Sin" (Heb. 10:12)—Christ's Death

209 The Good Shepherd
And His Sheep (John 10)

His Life is for their Ransom (v. 11)
His Voice is for their Call (v. 3)
His Gift is for their Salvation (v. 27)
His Hand is for their Preservation (v. 28)

210 The Wrath of God

The Reality of it (Job 36:18)
The Certainty of it (Rom. 1:18)
The Subjects of it (Col. 3:6)
The Duration of it (Rev. 14:10, 11)

211 Abundance of Good Things

Abundant Mercy (1 Peter 1:3)—to the Needy
Abundant Grace (1 Tim. 1:14)—to the Guilty
Abundant Life (John 10:10)—to the Dead
Abundant Satisfaction (Ps. 36:8)—to the Hungry

212   Voices of The Soul

"Behold, I am Vile" (Job 11:4)—A Convicted Sinner
"Behold God, my Salvation" (Isa. 12:2)—Believing Soul
"Behold what...Love" (1 John 3:1)—Happy Son

213   Divine Judgments

Judgment of the Sinner (Gen. 3:17-19)—Retribution
Judgment of the Sinbearer (Isa. 53:5)—Substitution
Judgment of the Saint (1 Peter 1:17)—Discipline
Judgment of the Servant (Rom. 14:10-12)—Review

1. Brought Condemnation on all the Race
2. Was a Ransom for all Mankind
3. Is a Present Experience of the Saved
4. A Manifestation of Works in the Future

214   The Cross of Christ

A Display of Human Hatred (Acts 4:26)
A Manifestation of Divine Love (1 John 3:10)
A Declaration of God's Righteousness (Rom. 3:25)
A Triumph over Satan's Power (Heb. 2)

1. Man's Probation is thereby Closed
2. God's Heart is therein Revealed
3. Heaven's Character is thus Cleared
4. Hell's Defeat is there Assured

215   Christ Work on Calvary,
And its Results to the World

He tasted Death for every Man (Heb. 2:9)
He gave Himself a Ransom for All (1 Tim. 2:6)
He procured Forgiveness for All (Acts 13:38)
He brought Salvation to All (1 Tim. 4:10)

1. Therefore Life is held forth for All (Rom. 6:23)
2. There is Deliverance preached to All (Luke 4:18)
3. Remission is within reach of All (Luke 10:43)
4. Present Salvation may be had by All (Titus 2:11)

216   Christ's Work on Calvary

Its Results to all Believers

He Redeemed them from all Iniquity (Titus 2:14)
He Purged them from all Sin (Heb. 1:3)
He Saved them from all Judgment (John 5:24)
He Delivered them from all Penalties (Gal. 3:13)

    1. His People are a Free People (John 8:36)
    2. His People are a Clean People (John 15:3)
    3. His People are a Justified People (Rom. 8:1)
    4. His People are a Redeemed People (Col. 1:14)

217   Glorious Things

In 1 Peter 1:1-6

Elect according to God's Foreknowledge (v. 2)
Cleansed by Sprinkling of Christ's Blood (v. 2)
Begotten unto a Living Hope (v. 3)
Kept for a Heavenly Inheritance (vv. 4, 5)

    The *First* is altogether of God
    The *Second* is made ours by Faith
    The *Third* is the Spirit's Work
    The *Fourth* is by the Power of God

218   Saved, to Worship Christ

The Leper who was Cleansed (Luke 17:15)
The Blind Man who got his Sight (John 9:38)
The Women...saved by Christ (Matt 28:9)
The Disciples who followed Christ (Luke 24:52)

219   Great Salvation

God's Grace is its Source (Eph. 2:5)
Christ's Death is its Cause (John 3:15)
Christ's Life is its Assurance (Rom. 5:9)
Christ's Coming is its Consummation (Heb. 10:28)

220   Certainties

Death—"Thou shall surely Die" (Gen. 2:17)
Substitution—"Surely He bore our Griefs" (Isa. 53:4)
Salvation—"Surely they are My People" (Isa. 63:8)
Supply—"Surely goodness..shall follow" (Ps. 23:6)
Hope—"Surely I come Quickly" (Rev. 22:20)

221   Great Days

Day of *Salvation* (2 Cor. 6:2)—When Jesus Saves
Day of *Redemption* (Eph. 4:30)—When Christ Comes
Day of *Wrath* (Rev. 6:17)—When Judgment Begins
Day of *Vengeance* (Isa 63:4)—When God Punishes

222   On the Cross

Sin was Put Away (Heb. 9:26)
Atonement was Made (1 John 2:2)
Reconciliation was Effected (Rom. 5:10)
Peace was Procured (Col. 1:20)

    1. Justification comes through Believing (Acts 13:39)
    2. It is Received by Faith (Rom. 5:11, Marg.)
    3. Remission is Preached in His Name (Acts 10:43)
    4. It is Enjoyed by the Justified (Rom. 5:1)

223   A Seated Christ

As Offerer of a Perfect Sacrifice (Heb. 10:12)
As Purger of His People's Sins (Heb. 1:4)
As High Priest Forever (Heb. 8:1)
As Perfecter of Faith's Path (Heb. 12:2)

224   Christ's Mighty Acts

He is the Life Giver (John 5:21)
He is the Liberator (John 8:36)
He is the Preserver (John 10:28)
He is the Receiver (John 14:3)

    1. He gives Life by His Voice (John 5:25)
    2. He gives Liberty through His Truth (John 8:32)
    3. He Preserves by His Life (Rom. 5:9)
    4. He Receives at His Coming (1 Thess. 4:17)

225 The Voice of Christ

Speaks

Life to the Dead (John 11:43, 44)
Pardon to the Guilty (Luke 7:48)
Peace to the Troubled (Luke 8:48)

226 Good Clothing

Garments of Salvation (Isa. 61:10)
Robe of Righteousness (Isa. 61:10)
White Raiment of Glory (Rev. 3:5)

    1. Provided by God's Grace (Titus 2:11)
    2. Procured by Christ's Death (Rom. 3:22)
    3. Awaiting the Saved in Glory (Rev. 7:14)

227 Christ's Three Gifts

He gave His *Love* at the Cross (Gal. 2:20)
He gives His *Life* from the Throne (John 17:2)
He gives His *Liberty* through the Gospel (Luke 4:18)

    1. His Love is to Believed (1 John 3:23)
    2. His Life is to be Received (John 3:36)
    3. His Liberty is to be Enjoyed (Gal. 5:1)

228 My God

God is my Salvation (Isa. 12:2)
God is my Strength (Ps. 43:2)
God is my Satisfier (Ps. 107:9)

    As Ruined Sinners we Need Salvation
    As Helpless and Weak we need Strength (Rom. 5:6)
    As Empty and Needy we need Satisfaction (Ps. 103:5)

229 Four Great Days

The Day of Salvation (Luke 19:9)
The Day of Death (Phil. 1:21)
The Day of Glorification (2 Thess. 1:10)
The Day of Judgment (2 Peter 1:9)

    1. The Beginning of Christian Life (2 Cor. 5:15)
    2. The Going to be with Christ (2 Cor. 5:8)
    3. The Being made like Christ (1 John 3:3)
    4. The Christ Rejecter's Doom (Rev. 20:11)

230   Four States of Man

In *Innocency* as Created (Gen. 1:26)
In *Sin* as Fallen (Rom. 3:10-16)
In *Grace* as Saved (Eph. 2:8)
In *Glory* as Perfected (1 John 3:2)

    The *First* will never be Regained
    The *Second* can never be Reformed
    The *Third* can now be Entered
    The *Fourth* will shortly be Revealed

231   Take

Take the Water of Life (Rev. 22:17)—Salvation
Take my Yoke (Matt. 11:29)—Submission
Take up the Cross (Mark 8:34)—Confession
Take the Armor of God (Eph. 6:13)—Conflict

    The Sinner's first necessity is Life
    The Saved One's surrender brings Liberty
    The Disciple shares in Reproach
    The Warrior stands for Victory

232   Sin, Concealed and Cancelled

Committing Sin brings Fear (Gen. 3:10)
Concealing Sin brings Misery (Prov. 28:13)
Confessing Sin brings Pardon (Luke 18:13, 14)
Cancelled Sin brings Peace (Rom. 5:1)

    Illustrated in Cain (Gen. 4:14); Adonijah (1 Kings 1:50)
    Proved by Achan (Josh 7:20, 21); Gehazi (2 Kings 5:27)
    Recorded of David (2 Sam. 12:13); the Publican (Luke 18:14)
    Witnessed in the Woman (Luke 7:50); the Eunuch (Acts 8:39)

233   Christ, A Mighty Savior
                       (Psalm 18:1-2)

A Firm Rock of Salvation (v. 2)—To Rest on
A Strong Fortress of Security (v. 2)—To Shelter in
A High Tower of Hope (v. 2)—To Look from

234 Christt Coming in Judgment
(Matthew 24)

It will be Swift as the Flash of Lightning (v. 27)
It will be Sudden as the Flood of Waters (v. 39)
It will be Secret as the Coming of a Thief (v. 43)

235 A Savior, Christ the Lord
(Luke 2:11)

A Divine Savior (John 1:1, 2)
A Human Savior (John 1:14)
A Crucified Savior (John 19:18)
A Risen Savior (John 20:19)

His Divine Person gives Value to His Work (Heb. 1:3)
His Perfect Manhood fits Him as Man's Deliverer (Heb. 2:14)
His Atoning Death, procures Man's Redemption (Heb. 9:12)
His Risen Life secures His people's Salvation (Rom. 5:9)

236 The Gospel of God
(Romans 1:1-16)

Its Source is "God" (v. 1)
Its Subject is "His Son" (v. 3)
Its Nature is "Power" (v. 16)
Its Object is "Salvation" (v. 16)

237 The Judgment of God
(Romans 2:1-8)

Its Certainty—"We are Sure" (v. 2)
Its Universality—"To every Man" (v. 6)
Its Righteousness—"According to Truth" (v. 2)
Its Results—"Indignation and Wrath" (v. 9)

The Judgment of God is Sure (Heb. 9:27)
It will be Full and Searching (Eccl. 11:9)
It will be Righteous and Just (Rev. 20:12, 13)
Its Results will be Final and Eternal (2 Peter 2:9)

238   Trees

Rooted up in Wrath (Jude 12)—Hypocrisy Exposed
Planted in Grace (Jer. 17:8)—Divine Life Imparted
Growing in Fruitfulness (Ps. 1:3)—Spiritual Progress
Cut Down in Judgment (Luke 13:7)—Sinner's Doom

239   Savior, Sacrifice, King:
Three Offices of The Lord Jesus

A Savior come from God to Man (John 3:17)
A Sacrifice offered Up to God for Man (Eph. 5:2)
A King enthroned to Rule Men for God (Heb. 1:8)

The *First* was Manifested in His Life (Luke 19:10)
The *Second* was Accomplished at His Death (Heb. 10:12)
The *Third* will be seen in His Kingdom (1 Cor. 15:28)

240   Abundance of Peace

Christ has made Peace (Col. 1:20)—By His Death
Christ preaches Peace (John 20:19)—In Resurrection
Christ is our Peace (Eph. 2:14)—In Exaltation
Christ Rules in Peace (Col. 3:15)—In the Heart

241   The Power of God

Manifest in the Sinner's Salvation (Rom. 1:16)
Exercised in the Saint's Preservation (1 Peter 1:5)
Displayed with Servant's Testimony (1 Cor. 2:4, 5)
Exhibited at the Church's Glorification (Phil. 3:20)

GREAT GOSPEL TEXTS

242   The Greatest Love Gift
(John 3:16)

A Wonderful Love—God so loved the World
A Matchless Gift—His only begotten Son
A Simple Way—Whosoever Believeth in Him
A Divine Certainty—Should not Perish
A Grand Possession—Have Everlasting Life

> The greatest Gospel text in the Bible
> Most used in the conversion of sinners
> Embracing God, Christ, sinners, salvation, damnation
> *Pray* over it, *possess* it afresh in *power*, then *preach* it

243   The Savior's Mission
(Luke 19:10)

His Name—The Son of Man
His Mission—Is Come to Seek
His Work—And to Save
His Object—That which was Lost

> The Person gives dignity and value to the work
> The Work is definite: not to *reform* but to *rescue*
> The Sinner is not merely *astray*, but *lost*

244   A Glorious Message
(Acts 16:31)

A Great Command—Believe on
A Glorious Person—The Lord Jesus Christ
A Grand Result—Thou shalt be Saved

Believing is *trust, reliance, committal* to
The Threefold Name, embracing Savior and Lord
A Present *possession* for personal enjoyment

245   Saved by Grace
(Ephesians 2:8)

The Cause—By Grace
The Certainty—Are ye Saved
The Channel—Through Faith
The Caution—Not of Yourselves
The Climax—The Gift of God

The *source* and *spring* of Salvation is God
The *assurance* and the *way* is by Faith
The *beginning* and *end* of all is—GOD

246   Sin and Its Removal
(Isaiah 53:6)

Universal Depravity—All gone Astray
Individual Perversity—Each takes his own Way
Divine Activity—Jehovah laid
Christ's Personality—On Him
Accepted Liability—Iniquity of us All

The *First* is charged in Rom. 5:12-19
The *Second* is proved in Rom. 3:10-17
The *Third* is declared in Rom. 3:25
The *Fourth* is announced in John 1:29
The *Fifth* is recorded in 1 Peter 2:24

247   A Personal Confession
(Isaiah 12:2)

Personal Acceptance—God is my Salvation
Individual Faith—I will Trust
Declared Assurance—And not be Afraid

Salvation is of, from, and in God (Titus 1:3)
Faith is reliance in, and on Christ (Eph. 1:13)
Assurance is derived from God's Word (1 John 5:13)

248   The Watchman and His Message
(Isaiah 21:11-12)

A Scorner's Question—What of the Night?
A Bright Morning of Glory—For the Saved
A Dark Night of Judgment—For Sinners
A Gospel Appeal to All—Return; Come

249   Life in a Look
(Isaiah 45:22)

A Simple Act—Look
A Divine Person—Unto Me
A Grand Assurance—Be ye Saved
A Wide Invitation—All ends of the Earth
An Only Savior—There is none else

250   Three Great Gospel Truths
(1 Peter 3:18)

Satisfaction—"Christ hath once suffered for Sins"
Substitution—"The Just for the Unjust"
Reconciliation—"That He might bring us to God"

The *atonement* of Christ makes *peace*
The *substitution* of Christ brings *salvation*
The *mediation* of Christ effects *reconciliation*

251   A Personal Question
(Hebrews 2:3)

A Searching Inquiry—How shall we Escape?
A Solemn Probability—If we Neglect
A Superb Provision—So great Salvation

> There will be no Escape (Heb. 12:25; 1 Thess. 5:3)
> Neglecters are as common as Rejecters (Luke 14:18)
> The Punishment is measured by the Gift despised (Heb. 10:29)

252   A Call to Decision
(1 Kings 18:21-39)

A Solemn Gathering (v. 19)—Day of Crisis
A Pointed Question (v. 21)—Personal to Each
A Great Issue (v. 21)—Nothing Between
A Definite Choice (v. 39)—Grand Decision

> There are such Times in all Lives (Matt. 27:22)
> There is great Danger in Delay (Acts 24:25)
> There is no Neutrality Possible (Matt. 6:24)
> The Life Choice is then made (Ruth 1:16, 17)

253   A Sinner Forgiven
(Psalm 32:1)

The Need of Forgiveness (Rom. 3:23)
The Cause of Forgiveness (Acts 13:38)
The Fulness of Forgiveness (Col. 2:13)
The Blessedness of Forgiveness (Rom. 4:7)

> Guilt Owned and Confessed is the Condition (Rom. 3:19)
> Christ's Atoning Death is the Cause (Rom. 3:25)
> Faith's Acceptance brings it in Full (Acts 13:39)
> Peace and Joy are the Result (Rom. 5:1-2)

254   The Sinner's Surety
(Isaiah 53:5)

The Wounded Surety (1 Peter 3:18)—Suffered for us
The Bruised Sinbearer (Gal. 3:13)—Bore our Curse
The Procurer of Peace (Col. 1:20)—By His Blood
The Healer of our Woe (Job 20:20)—By His Wounds

255   An Invitation to the Weary
(Matthew 11:28)

A Great Invitation—Come unto Me
A Laboring People—Workers for Salvation
A Burdened Heart—Convicted of Sin
A Present Release—Rest from and in Christ
>The Person of Christ is the only Rest-giver
>The Work of Christ is the true Resting-place
>The Spirit convicts of Sin and leads to Christ
>Faith responds to the Call and comes to Christ

256   Salvation, Liberty, Satisfaction
(John 10:9)

Access—I am THE Door
Acceptance—If any Man enter in
Salvation—He shall be Saved
Liberty—Go In and Out
Satisfaction—And find Pasture

257   From the Pit to the Song
(Psalm 40:1-3)

The Sinner's Fallen Position—In a Pit
The Savior's Mighty Power—Brought me Up
The Saved Sinner's Place—Set on a Rock
The Happy Saint's Praise—A New Song

258   Wages and the Gift
(Romans 6:23)

Sin's Wages is our Due (James 1:15; Rom. 6:21)
Death is Distance from God (Rom. 5:12; Rev. 20:14)
God's Gift of Love and Life (John 3:16; 10:10)
Received and Enjoyed Now (John 1:12; 1 John 5:12)
Refused or Rejected by Many (John 5:40; Acts 13:46)

259 The Life That Is Worth Living
(1 Timothy 4:8)

It is Begun at New Birth (1 John 5:1)
It is Manifest in a new Walk (Rom. 6:4)
It is Provided for by Divine Power (2 Peter 2:3)
It is Lived in Hope of coming Glory (Titus 2:12, 13)

260 A Great Proclamation
(Acts 13:38-39)

A Divine Edict—Be it Known
A Great Mediator—Through this Man
A Definite Message—Is Preached unto You
A Wonderful Amnesty—Forgiveness of Sins
A Specified Number—All that Believe
A Full Remission—Are Justified from all Things

It Comes with the full Authority of Heaven
Its Procuring Cause, the Person and Work of Christ
A Proclamation is more than a Promise
This Forgiveness is the Result of a Ransom
It is for All, but Possessed only by Believers
Justification exceeds as it includes Forgiveness

261 Grace in Action
(Titus 2:11-12)

Divine Favor—The Grace of God
Its True Character—Salvation—Bringing
Its Present Aspect—Hath Appeared
Its World Wide Attitude—To all Men
Its Training of the Saved—Teaching Us
Its Practical Lessons—Denying Ungodliness, etc.
Its Happy Prospect—Looking for that Blessed Hope

Grace brings Salvation to the Lost
Grace Disciplines those who are Saved
Grace sets before them the Hope of Glory

262   Death Disarmed
(Hebrews 2:9, 14, 15)

"The Power of Death" was in Satan's Hand
"The Fear of Death" was the Sinner's Bondage
"The Suffering of Death," the Savior's Experience
"Deliverance from Death" is the Saint's Victory

> By the Fall of Man, the Devil gained this Power
> In the Conscience of Man, the Dread of Death Abides
> By the Cross of Christ, the Devil is Disarmed
> In the Victory of Christ, His people are Delivered

263   Three Manifestations of Christ
(Hebrews 9:24-28)

As Sacrifice and Sinbearer—He *has* Appeared
As Representative and Advocate—He *now* Appears
As Savior and Glorifier—He *shall* Appear

> The Perfect Sacrifice of Christ brings us unto God
> His Priesthood and Advocacy maintain us with God
> His Coming will Introduce us to the Glory of God

264   God's Unspeakable Gift
(2 Corinthians 9:15)

The Gift has already been Given (John 3:16)
The Gift is to be Personally Received (John 1:12)
The Gift may be Definitely Possessed (1 John 5:12)
The Gift can be Foolishly Rejected (Matt. 21:38)

265   Soul-damning Sins
(2 Thessalonians 2:11, 12; Mark 16:16)

The Son of God Rejected (Heb. 10:29)
The Spirit of God Despised (Heb. 10:29)
The Word of God Disbelieved (1 John 5:10)

> The Sacrifice of Christ Despised, brings Punishment
> The Spirit Resisted, brings judicial Hardness of Heart
> The Truth of God Rejected, the Devil's Lie is Received

266   The Lord's Jewels
(Malachi 3:17)
His, because He Sought Them (Matt. 13:44)
His, because He Bought Them (Matt. 13:46)
His, therefore He Claims Them (Titus 2:14)
His, therefore He will Gather Them (2 Thess. 2:1)

267   Justified Freely
(Romans 3:24-26)
Justification by Grace (v. 24)—The Source
Propitiation by Blood (v. 25)—The Channel
Appropriation by Faith (v. 26)—The Means
    The Sovereign Grace of God is its Cause
    The Atoning Death of Christ is its Conveyance
    The Sinner's Faith is its Acceptance

268   Christ, Our Ransom
(1 Timothy 2:5, 6)
Man has no Ransom (Ps. 49:7)
God has found a Ransom (Job 33:24)
Christ gave His Life a Ransom (Matt. 20:28)
    His Ransom avails for All Men (1 Tim. 2:16)
    The Gospel for All is the Testimony to It (1 Tim. 2:4, 5)
    After Death it does not Avail (Job 36:18)

269   A Genuine Revival
(Acts 11:19-24)
Preachers go Forth into New Fields—The Grecians
The Theme of their Preaching—The Lord Jesus
The Power with Them—The Hand of the Lord
The Result, Inwardly—A Number Believed
The Manifestation, Outwardly—Turned to the Lord

270 Sure Testimonies
(Psalm 19:7)

A Sure Foundation (2 Tim. 2:17)—To Rest upon
A Sure Anchor (Heb. 6:19)—To Hold by
A Sure Word (2 Peter 1:20)—To Guide us
A Sure Dwelling Place (Isa. 32:18)—Awaiting us

> The Foundation of God can never be Moved
> The Anchor of God can never be Uplifted
> The Word of God can never be Broken
> The Home of God can never be Forfeited

271 Precious Faith
(2 Peter 1:1)

The Word of Faith (Rom. 10:8)—Christ's Work
The Object of Faith (Eph. 1:13)—Christ's Person
The Basis of Faith (Rom. 10:17)—God's Word
The Result of Faith (Eph. 2:8)—Man's Salvation

272 The Righteousness of God
(Romans 10:2-3)

Its Revelation in the Gospel (Rom. 3:21)
Its Purpose, that God might be Just (Rom. 3:26)
Its Appropriation by Man's Faith (Rom. 3:22)
Its Rejection by the Self-righteous (Rom. 10:3)

273 Human Guilt
(Romans 3:9-20)

The Great Indictment (v. 9)
The Case Proved (vv. 10-18)
The Final Verdict (v. 19)
The Culprit Hopeless (v. 20)

> God, as Moral Governor, frames the Charge
> Law and Prophets prove the Sinner's Guilt
> The Accused Condemned and Silenced
> By no Efforts of his, can he gain Freedom

274 Righteousness Imputed & Imparted
(Romans 4:6)

Righteousness is Imputed to Believers (Rom. 4:3)
Righteousness is Imparted at New Birth (Eph. 4:24)
Righteousness Manifested in New Life (1 John 3:10)

The *First* is the Believer's Standing
The *Second* is the Believer's State
The *Third* is the Evidence of Sonship

275 Three Reigning Powers
(Romans 5:17-21)

The Reign of Sin (v. 21)—The Sinner's Conquest
The Reign of Grace (v. 21)—God's Triumph
The Reign in Life (v. 17)—The Saint's Victory

276 The Sinner Described
(Romans 5:6-9)

"Ungodly" (v. 6), Alienated—His State
"Sinners" (v. 8), Activity—His Acts
"Enemies" (v. 9), Depravity—His Nature

The *First* is the Fruit
The *Second* is the Branch
The *Third* is the Root

277 God's Answer to Man's Need
(Job 33:24)

A Ransom from God is Provided (1 Tim. 2:5,6)
The Grace of God is Manifested (Titus 2:2)
The Power of God is Exercised (Rom. 1:16)

The Ransom has been Given and Accepted
The Grace is Full and Unreserved
The Power is Waiting to give Deliverance

278   Christ, the Bread of Life
(John 6:51)

His Character—Living Bread
His Origin—Came from Heaven
His Mission—To give Life
His Invitation—If any Man eat
His Promise—Shall Live Forever

All have Existence, but not Spiritual Life (1 Tim. 5:6)
Life is in Christ and from Christ (John 10:10)
It is Received by Sinners through Believing (John 20:31)
It is Manifested in a New Walk (Rom. 6:4)

279 Man's Destitution: God's Provision
(Hosea 13:9)

He has no Life (John 6:53)
He has no Peace (Isa. 57:21)
He has no Hope (Eph. 2:12)

Christ has made Peace by His Cross (Col. 1:20)
Christ has brought Life through His Death (John 20:31)
Christ is the Hope of His People (1 Tim. 1:1)

280   "It is Finished"
(John 19:30)

"It"—The Work the Father gave Him (John 17:4)
"Is"—Not in Progress, but done forever (Heb. 10:12)
"Finished"—Completed and Perfected (Heb. 10:18)

The Claims of God have been fully Met
The Work to be done has been wholly Finished
Nothing can be added, nor will anything be Accepted

281   A Triple Invitation
(Isaiah 55:3)

"Incline your Ear" (Rom. 10:17)—Hearing of Faith
"Come unto Me" (Rom. 1:5)—Obedience of Faith
"Hear and Live" (John 5:24)—Life through Faith

282   Christ "The Way"
(John 14:6)

He Himself is the Way—His Person
He opened the Way to God (Heb. 10:12)—His Work
He is the Door of Salvation (John 10:9)—For the Lost
He is the Way of Access (Eph. 2:18)—To the Saved
He is the Way to the Throne (Heb. 10:20)—In Glory

> "Some other Way" (John 10:1), is contrary to God
> "Man's own Way" (Prov. 14:12), leads to Death
> God's "Narrow Way" (Matt. 7:14), leads to Life

283   An Old Time Conversion
(Psalm 13:5, 6)

God's Mercy Accepted (v. 5)
God's Salvation Rejoiced In (v. 5)
God's Praises Sung (v. 6)
God's Bounty Testified Of (v. 6)

> The Mercy of God is the Sinner's Trust (Eph. 2:4)
> The Salvation of God, the Believer's Joy (Ps. 9:14)
> The Praise of God is His Song (Ps. 40:3)
> To show forth His Virtues, his Work (1 Peter 2:9)

284   Forgers of Lies
(Job 13:4)

The Devil (Gen. 3:4)—"Ye shall not surely Die"
The Antichrist (1 John 2:22)—Denies the Son
The Atheist (Ps. 14:2)—"There is no God"
The New Theologian (2 Peter 2:2)—No Atonement
The Scoffer (2 Peter 3:3, 4)—There is no Judgment

285   Safe Keeping
(Isaiah 26:3)

The Mighty Keeper—"Thou wilt Keep"
The Way He Keeps—"In Perfect Peace"
The Attitude of the Kept—"Whose Mind is Stayed"
The Object of Faith—"He Trusteth in Thee"

286   Become Unprofitable
(Romans 3:12)
Man in his Ruined State is described as
Altogether become Filthy (Ps. 14:3)
His Heart is Desperately Wicked (Jer. 17:9)
His Righteousness is as Filthy Rags (Isa. 64:6)
His Religion is an Abomination (Isa. 1:13)
He needs to be "Born Again" (John 3:3)

287   Emmanuel, "God With Us"
(Matthew 1:23)
To Manifest God's Love in Life (1 John 4:9)
Declare God's Righteousness in Death (Rom. 3:25)
To Mediate between God and Man (1 Tim. 2:5)
To Reconcile Men to God (2 Cor. 5:19)
> The Excellency of Christ's Person
> The Value of Christ's Work
> The Acceptance of Christ's Atonement
> The Results to All who Believe

288   The Son of Man's Mission
(Matthew 20:28)
The Name of His Humiliation—"Son of Man"
His Definite Mission—"He Came"
His Personal Activity—"To Serve and Give"
His Atoning Death—"A Ransom for Many"
> Incarnation was Essential to His death (Heb. 2:14)
> Sent by the Father, He came (John 3:17)
> Not to Get but to Give (John 10:11)
> His Ransom is Sufficient for All (1 Tim. 2:6)
> Efficient only in them that Believe (Acts 13:39)

289   "Precious Blood"
(1 Peter 1:9)

It Redeems from Sin's Power (Eph. 1:7)
It Justifies from Sin's Guilt (Rom. 5:9)
It Releases from Sin's Bondage (Rev. 1:5)
It Cleanses from Sin's Defilement (1 John 1:7)

"Blood" is the Symbol of Life given to God (Lev. 17:11)
Not the Life lived, but poured forth in Death (Matt. 26:28)
Apart from Blood-shedding is no Remission (Heb. 9:22)
Christ's Sacrifice is past: its Results remain (Heb. 10:12)

290   The Cross of Christ
(Galatians 6:12)

The Death of the Cross (Phil. 2:8)—Its Shame
Reconciliation of the Cross (Eph. 2:16)—Its Results
The Endurance of the Cross (Heb. 12:2)—Its Penalty
The Word of the Cross (1 Cor. 1:18)—Its Message
Crucifixion at the Cross (Gal. 6:14)—Its Acceptance

291   Deliverance to the Captives
(Luke 4:18)

From the Power of Darkness (Col. 1:13)—Satan's Rule
From Wrath to Come (1 Thess. 1:10)—Sin's Penalty
From the Law's Claims (Rom. 7:6)—Our Due
From the Present Evil World (Gal. 1:4)—Our Course

292   Great Redemption
(Psalm 111:9)

A Great Redeemer (Jer. 50:34)—The Lord Jesus
A Sacrificial Redemption (Eph. 1:7)—By His Blood
A Sure Possession (Col. 1:14)—Believers have it
Its Present Object (Titus 2:14)—From all Iniquity
Its Future Purpose (Rom. 8:23)—Our Bodies
Its Ultimate End (Rev. 5:9)—Unto God

293   "I Obtained Mercy"
(1 Timothy 1:13, 16)

Who? A Blasphemer and Persecutor (v. 13)
Where? "In Christ Jesus" (v. 14)
Why? That all Long-suffering be Shown (v. 16)
What For? As a Pattern to Others (v. 16)

> The Result: Saul was Saved and sent to Preach
> The Lesson: None need Despair, Chief of Sinners is Saved
> The Message: Christ came to Save Sinners (v.15)

294   "All Things Are Now Ready"
(Luke 14:17)

Salvation is Prepared (Luke 2:30, 31; Acts 28:28)
Forgiveness Procured and Proclaimed (Acts 13:38)
Peace Purchased and Preached (Col. 1:20; Acts 10:36)

> The Day of Salvation is NOW (2 Cor. 6:2)
> God's Forgiveness is to be Received (Acts 26:18)
> Peace is Possessed by the Believer (Rom. 5:1)

295   The Savior Presented
(Isaiah 53:2-11)

A Tender Plant (v. 2)—Babe of Bethlehem
Rejected of Men (v. 3)—The Nazarene
Man of Sorrows (v. 3)—In His Ministry
Smitten of God (v. 4)—Our Surety
Bearing Our Curse (v. 5)—Our Substitute
Putting Away Sin (v. 6)—Our Sinbearer
Raised from the Dead (v. 11)—Our Justifier

296   Saving Faith
(Luke 7:50)

It comes by Hearing of Christ (Rom. 10:17)
It brings its Need to Christ (Matt. 15:28)
It gets into Touch with Christ (Mark 5:27)
It reposes on the Word of Christ (John 4:50)
It receives Salvation from Christ (Luke 7:50)

297   Christt Delivered and Raised

(Romans 4:25)

He gave Himself for our Sins (Gal. 1:4)
He gave His Life a Ransom (Matt. 20:28)
He Bore our Sins on The Tree (1 Peter 2:24)
He Died for our Sins (1 Cor. 15:3)

> All being Fulfilled, God Raised Him (Acts 13:30)
> Resurrection is the Seal of Acceptance (1 Cor. 15:17)
> And the Sign of Sin put Away (1 Cor. 15:17)

298 Eternal Life, a Present Assurance

It is God's free Gift in Christ (Rom 6:23)
To Receive Christ is to get Life (John 1:12, 13)
To Have Christ is to have Life (1 John 5:12)

> The Knowledge of this is through the Word (1 John 5:13)
> The Enjoyment of it is by the Spirit (Rom. 7:2)
> The Manifestation of it is in the Walk (Rom. 6:6)

299   A Just God and a Savior

(Isaiah 45:22)

God is Just (Deut. 32:4)
Christ is the Just One (Acts 22:14)
Sinners are Unjust (2 Peter 2:9)

> Christ Suffered the Just for the Unjust (1 Peter 3:18)
> God is Just and the Justifier (Rom. 3:26)
> He is Faithful and Just to Forgive (1 John 1:9)

300   The Great Peacemaker

(Isaiah 53:5)

Peace Announced at His Birth (Luke 2:14)
Peace Pronounced in His Ministry (Mark 5:34)
Peace Procured by His Death (Col. 1:20)
Peace Preached in His Resurrection (John 20:19)
Peace Secured in His Exaltation (Eph. 2:14)
Peace Reigns in His Kingdom (Isa. 54:10)

301   A Living Redeemer
(Job 19:25)

A Redeemer Needed (Ps. 49:7)
A Redeemer Provided (Isa. 47:4)
A Redemption Procured (Heb. 9:12)
The Redeemer Exalted (Rev. 5:9)

302   Sin's Removal
(Psalm 103:12)

Sin Rests on the Sinner (Isa. 1:4)
Sins Separate the Soul from God (Isa. 59:2)
Christ put away Sin by His Sacrifice (Heb. 9:26)
Christ Purged our Sins by His Blood (Heb. 1:3)
Sin's Remission proclaimed in Gospel (Acts 10:43)
Sins Forgiven for His Name's Sake (1 John 2:12)

303   The Sinner's Cleansing
(Psalm 51:7)

Man is Polluted and Unclean (Isa. 64:6)
He cannot cleanse Himself (Job 9:30)
No human devices cleanse from Sin (Jer. 2:22)
Atonement to God procures Cleansing (Lev. 16:30)
     Christ's Death Appropriated, Cleanses (Rev. 1:5)
     The Believing Sinner is Washed (1 Cor. 6:2)
     He is already Meet for Heaven (Col. 1:12)

304   The Song of the Forgiven
(Psalm 103:1-5)

Salvation first, its Song after (Exod. 14:30; 15:1)
Praise for Iniquities Forgiven (v. 3, with Isa. 44:22)
Thanks for Diseases Healed (v. 3, with Ps. 107:20)
Joy for a Life Redeemed (v. 4, with 1 Peter 1:18)
Song of a Soul Satisfied (v. 4, with Ps. 36:8)

305   Salvation and Its Song
(Isaiah 13:4)

God's Anger turned Away (v. 1)—At the Cross
Salvation brought Near (v. 2)—In the Gospel
Living Water flowing Forth (v. 3)—By the Spirit
Praise Going Up (v. 4)—From the Saved

> The Judgment of Sin was on Christ (Gal. 3:13)
> Salvation by Grace is Received by Faith (Eph. 2:8)
> The Spirit Indwells and Flows from the Saved (John 4:7)
> Praise goes Up, and Testimony goes Forth (1 Peter 2:5, 9)

306   An Indictment and a Pardon
(Isaiah 43:23-25)

God's Claims Disowned (v. 23)—Omission
God's Law Transgressed (v. 24)—Commission
God's Pardon Proclaimed (v. 26)—Remission

> That which is God's Due is Denied Him (Deut. 6:4, 5)
> That which He Forbids has been Done (James 1:10)
> Grace forgives Freely, and pardons Abundantly (Isa. 55:7)

VITAL SOUL-SEARCHING QUESTIONS

307 How Many Are Mine Iniquities?
(Job 13:23)
Our Transgressions are Multiplied (Isa. 59:12)
Christ Died for our Sins (1 Cor. 15:3)
The Lord laid on Him all our Iniquity (Isa. 53:6)
Christ Bare our Sins in His Own Body (1 Peter 2:24)
I am He that blotteth. . . Transgressions (Isa. 43:25)
Remission to Whosoever believeth in Him (Acts 10:43)
Sins and Iniquities remembered No More (Heb. 10:17)

308 What Shall a Man Give in Exchange for His Soul?
(Mark 8:37)
Not the *World*, for it "Passeth Away" (1 John 2:17)
Not his *Wealth*, for it "Profiteth Not" (Prov. 11:4)
Not his *Honor*, for it "Perisheth" (Ps. 49:12)
The Lord Alone can Deliver the Soul (Ps. 116:8)
He Alone is the Soul's Salvation (Ps. 35:3)

309 Wherewith Shall I Come Before the Lord?
(Micah 6:6)
Not with my Righteousness: It is Unclean (Isa. 44:5)
Not with my Religion: It is Unacceptable (Mic. 3:4)
Not with my Works: They are Dead (Heb. 9:14)
As a Sinner Confessed: Trusting (Luke 18:13)
Guilty before God, to be Justified (Rom. 3:19-23)
As Believing in Christ for Salvation (Rom. 10:9)

310   Do You Know the Lord?

Pharaoh—"I know not the Lord" (Exod. 5:2)
Paul—"I know whom I have believed" (2 Tim. 1:12)
"This is life eternal that they might know Thee, the only true God, and
Jesus Christ whom Thou hast sent" (John 17:3).

311   Are You Saved?

"Who *hath* Saved us" (2 Tim. 1:9)
"Who are *being* Saved" (Heb. 7:25)
"We *shall* be Saved" (Rom. 5:9)

> The *First* is Salvation in *Possession*, from Christ Crucified
> The *Second* is Salvation in *Progression*, from Christ Risen
> The *Third* is Salvation in *Prospect*, at Christ's Coming

312   Do You Know Your Sins
Are Forgiven?

Forgiveness was *Procured* at the Cross (Eph. 1:7)
Forgiveness is *Proclaimed* in the Gospel (Acts 13:38)
Forgiveness is *Received* through Believing (Acts 10:44)
Forgiveness is *Assured* by the Word (Eph. 4:32)
Forgiveness is *Enjoyed* in His Name (1 John 2:12)

313   Are You at Peace With God?

There is no Peace to the Wicked (Isa. 57:21)
Way of Peace is Unknown to Sinners (Rom. 3:17)
Christ has made Peace by His Blood (Col. 1:20)
The Gospel preaches Peace by Jesus (Acts 10:36)
The Believing Soul has Peace with God (Rom. 5:1)

314   What Must I Do to Be Saved?
(Acts 16:30-31)

Believe on the Lord Jesus Christ. . .shalt be Saved
By Grace are ye Saved, through Faith (Eph. 2:8)
According to His Mercy He Saved us (Titus 3:5)
It pleased God to save them that Believe (1 Cor. 1:21)

315 How Doth God Know?
(Job 22:13)

His Eyes are in every Place (Prov. 15:3)
His Eyes are on the Ways of Man (Job 34:21)
Their Secret Sins are all before Him (Ps. 90:8)
He Knoweth the Secrets of the Heart (Ps. 44:21)
God shall Judge Man's Secrets (Rom. 2:16)
He will bring every Secret to Judgment (Eccl. 12:14)
He Knoweth Them that Trust in Him (Nah. 1:7)
The Lord Knoweth Them that are His (2 Tim. 2:19)

316 How Shall Man Be Just With God?
(Job 9:2)

There is not a Just Man on Earth (Eccl. 7:20)
There is None Righteous, no not One (Rom. 3:10)
Not the Hearers of the Law are Justified (Rom. 2:13)
By Works shall no Man be Justified (Rom. 3:20)
Christ Died, the Just for the Unjust (1 Peter 3:18)
Believers are Justified by His Blood (Rom. 5:9)
All that Believe are Justified (Acts 13:39)
God Justifieth. Who Condemneth? (Rom. 8:33)

317 Who Shall Be Able to Stand?
(Revelation 6:17)

Not the Sinner (Ps. 130:3)—He will Shrink
Not the Hypocrite (Isa. 33:14)—He will Fear
Not the Proud (Jer 48:42, 44)—He will Flee
Not the Rich (Rev. 6:15, 16)—He will Quail
Only the Christian (Rom. 14:4)—He is "in Christ"

"On Christ, the solid Rock, I stand,
All other ground is sinking sand."

318   Where Shall I spend Eternity?

There is a Heaven of Eternal Glory for the Saved
And a Hell of Eternal Woe for the Lost
Without Holiness, no Man shall see the Lord
Apart from New Birth, none enter the Kingdom
To be "*in* Christ" now, is to be "*with* Christ" then
To Die in Sins is to be shut out from Christ

Rev. 21:3;   Heb. 12:14;   Phil. 1:13, 23
Mark 9:47, 48;   John 3:3;   John 8:21

319 If a Man Die, Shall He Live Again?
(Job 14:14)

All in the Graves shall come forth (John 5:28)
Some to a Resurrection of Life (John 5:29)
Some to a Resurrection of Judgment (John 5:29)
The Saved for Eternal Glory (1 Cor. 15:43)
The Lost to Everlasting Contempt (Dan. 12:2)

320   Why Will Ye Die?
(Ezekiel 33:11)

There is Life in Christ for All (John 5:26)
God is Giving it to All (Rom. 6:23)
The Way of Life is Simple (John 5:25)
The Possession of Life is Sure (1 John 5:12)
The Prospect of Life is Glorious (Rom. 6:22)
The Rejection of Life is Ruinous (Acts 13:46)

321 What Is Man That Thou Shouldest Set Thine Heart Upon Him?
(Job 7:17)

He was Formed in God's Image (Gen. 1:27)
He is Fallen from His Innocence (Rom. 5:12)
He is the Enemy of God (Rom. 5:9)
He is the Murderer of Christ (Acts 7:52)
Yet He is the Object of God's Love (John 3:16)

FAMILIAR GOSPEL TEXTS

322   The Blood on the Houses
(Exodus, Chapters 11 and 12)
A Night of Judgment (Exod. 11:5, 12:29)
A Substitute Provided (12:3-5)
The Lamb Slain (12:6)
The Blood Applied (12:7, 22)
The Word of Assurance (12:13, 23)

> The Judgment of the World will so Come (1 Thess. 5:2-10)
> The Lamb Provided and set Apart (John 1:29)
> Christ, our Passover, Sacrificed for Us (1 Cor. 5:7)
> Faith Appropriates the Sacrifice (Rom. 3:25)
> The Word of Christ assures Believers (John 5:24)

323   The Serpent on the Pole
(Numbers 21:1-11)
Sin Committed against God (v. 5)
Judgment follows from God (v. 6)
Sin Confessed to God (v. 7)
A Remedy provided from God (v. 8)
A Way prescribed by God (v. 8)
New Life imparted from God (v. 9)

> Sin brings Death (Rom. 6:23)
> Christ Crucified brings Life (John 3:14)
> Life is in a Look (Isa. 45:22)
> Known by the Word (1 John 5:12)

324   The Ark and Its Inmates
(Genesis 6, 7)
Coming Judgment Announced (Gen. 6:12, 13)
Noah believed the Warning (Heb. 11:7)
An Ark provided according to God (Gen. 6:14)
God's Invitation to enter, Obeyed (Gen. 7:1)
Noah's Security in God's hand (Gen. 6:16)
All Saved to go forth to Worship (Gen. 8:18, 20)

2 Peter 3:5-10	John 1:14	John 10:28
Rom. 3:4	John 10:9	1 Thess. 4:14

325   Passage of the Red Sea
(Exodus 14:13-31)
The People shut in and Helpless (v. 3, 9)
The Enemy Strong and Defiant (v. 10; 15:9)
The Salvation of God Revealed (vv. 13, 27)
Faith's Acceptance of It (vv. 22, 31)
Israel's Enjoyment of It (Exod. 15:1-2)

     Rom. 5:6; Acts 26:18; Acts 28:28; Isa. 12:2; Ps. 27:1

326   The Rebel Son
Law and Grace Contrasted (Deut. 21:18, with Luke 15:20-23)
We are Rebels All (Isa. 1:2)
All are Disobedient (Titus 3:3)
Refusing to Hearken (Ps. 81:11)
Liable to Judgment (Rom. 3:19)
Law enacts the Penalty (Rom. 6:23)
Grace Welcomes and Forgives (Isa. 55:7)
Grace Clothes and Crowns (Ps. 103:1, 5)

327   Water From the Rock
(Exodus 17:1-7; 1 Corinthians 10:4)

The People Athirst (John 4:14)—The Soul's Need
The Rock Provided (Neh. 9:15)—God's Provision
The Rock Smitten (Isa. 53:5)—Christ's Death
The Water Flowing (John 10:11)—Life Abundant
Free for All (Isa. 55:1)—Life without Price
Accessible to All (Rev. 22:17)—"Whosoever Will"

328   Accepted in His Offering
(Leviticus 1:1-9)

Burnt Offering (Eph. 5:2)—Christ's Sacrifice Godward
Perfect, Spotless (1 Peter 1:19)—Christ's Personal Worth
All Offered to God (Heb. 9:14)—Christ's Surrender
Identification (Gal. 2:20)—Faith's Acceptance
Worth Transferred (Eph. 1:6)—Believer's Acceptance

329   The Sin-offering Gospel
(Leviticus 4:27-35)

Unblemished Sacrifice (2 Cor. 5:20)—Christ Sinless
Offered for Sinners (Rom. 5:8)—Christ's Death for us
Hand laid on Head (John 1:29)—Faith's View of Christ
Blood Sprinkled (Rom. 3:25)—Christ our Propitiation
Sins Forgiven (Acts 10:43)—Assured by the Word

330   Priests Cleansed and Clothed
(Leviticus 8:1-10; Exodus 29)

Taken Out (Eph. 1:4)—God's Election by Grace
Brought to Door (1 Peter 1:2)—Spirit's Setting Apart
Washed with Water (Titus 3:5)—Regeneration
Clothed, Beautiful (1 Cor. 1:30)—Believer "in Christ"
Crowned and Anointed (1 Peter 2:5)—Priestly Place

The whole producing a wonderful picture of the believing sinner, chosen, cleansed, clothed, crowned, and consecrated as a worshiper of and worker for God.

331   The Leper and His Cleansing
(Leviticus 13:45; 14:1)

Leper pronounced Unclean (Isa. 1:6)—Sin in the Nature
Place "afar off" (Eph. 2:12)—The Sinner's Position
The Priest goes Forth (1 Tim. 1:15)—Christ's Mission
Sacrifice Offered (1 Cor. 15:3)—Christ Died for Sin
Live Bird Loosed (Rom. 4:25)—Christ Releases us
Water Sprinkled (John 15:3)—Word of Cleansing
Clothes Washed (Col. 3:8)—Practical Sanctification

332   The First Fruits Sheaf
(Leviticus 23:9-22; 1 Corinthians 15:20)

Honored Day (Matt.28:1)—Resurrection Morn
A Sheaf Reaped (Col. 1:18)—Christ, the First-born
Waved before Jehovah (John 12:24)—Acceptance
Harvest Accepted (Eph. 1:6)—Believer's Acceptance

Christ's Resurrection seals our Justification (Rom. 4:25)
Christ's Triumph, the Sign of our Victory (1 Cor. 15:57)
Christ's Exaltation, the Pledge of our Reign (2 Tim. 2:11)
Christ's Glorification, the Certainty of Ours (Rom. 8:17)

333   The Budding Rod
(Numbers 17:1-12)

Twelve Rods Tested (Gal. 3:21)—Man's Trial
Chosen Rod Buds (1 Peter 2:16)—Christ, God's Elect
Budded Rod Honored (Heb. 2:9)—Christ's Exaltation
Pledge of Glorification (Heb. 6:20)—Forerunner
Judgment Sure (Acts 17:31)—Christ, the Judge

334   The Cleansing Water
(Numbers 19:1-12)

Heifer Chosen (1 Peter 1:20)—Christ, the Chosen Victim
Blood Shed and Sprinkled (Heb. 10:12)—His Atonement
Ashes Preserved (1 John 1:7)—Value of Christ's Work
Water of Separation (Eph. 5:26)—Word used by Christ
Continuous Use (Ps. 119:9)—Believer's Responsibility

335   The Dried-up River
(Joshua 3:1-17)

Jordan's River (Heb. 9:27)—Figure of Judgment
Jordan's Swelling (Jer. 12:4)—Sinner meeting Death
The Ark Enters (Isa. 53:5)—Christ, our Surety
The Waters Cut off (Heb. 2:14)—Death Disarmed
A Passage Opened (John 14:6)—Christ, our Life
Living Priest (Heb. 6:19-20)—Christ, our Security

336   The Twelve Stones
(Joshua 4:1-9)

Twelve Stones in Jordan (Eph. 2:1)—Man dead in sins
Raised up (Eph. 2:5, 6)—Resurrection Life in Christ
Seated in Canaan (Eph. 2:6)—The Believer's Position
Sign and Witness (Col. 3:1)—His Life and Testimony
Twelve Stones Buried (Rom. 6:6, 19)—Old Man's End

337   The Scarlet Line
(Joshua 2:1-21; 6:25)

A True Token, v. 12 (Ps. 49:7)—The Sinner's Need
The Scarlet Cord (Ps. 22:6)—Christ's Atoning Death
Bound in Window, v. 18 (Rom. 3:25)—Faith in Blood
Word Pledged, v. 19 (Heb. 6:18)—God's Assurance
The Promise Fulfilled, 6:25 (1 Thess. 1:10)—Safe
The Living Witness (Eph. 2:19)—Citizen of Heaven

338   The Sinner Found Out
(Joshua 7:1-26)

Sin Committed, v. 1, 21 (James 1:15)—Course of Sin
Sin Concealed, v. 21 (Prov. 28:13)—Covering of Sin
Sin Unearthed, v. 22 (Num. 32:23)—Confrontation
Sin's Retribution, v. 25 (Col. 3:6)—Condemnation

339   A Safe Hiding Place
(Isaiah 32:1-2)
A Man (1 Tim. 2:5—The Man, Christ Jesus
Hiding Place (Ps. 32:7)—The Sinner's Refuge
Covert (Ps. 61:4)—The Believer's Security
Rivers (John 7:37)—The Soul's Refreshment
Shadow (Song of Sol. 2:3)—The Saint's Delight
A Robe of Righteousness (Isa. 61:10—For the Guilty

340   Cisterns and the Fountain
(Jeremiah 2:13)
Broken Cisterns (Heb. 11:25)—The Pleasures of Sin
Hewed Out (John 4:13)—Man's Helpless Efforts
The True Fountain (Ps. 36:9)—God in Christ
Living Waters (John 7:37)—Christ's Fulness
Full and Free (John 4:14; Rev. 22:17)—To All

341   The Potter and His vessel
(Jeremiah 8:1-4)
The Potter's at Work (Gen. 1:1)—God the Creator
The Vessel Made (Gen. 1:26)—Man in Innocence
The Vessel Marred (Eccl. 7:29)—Man Ruined by Sin
The Vessel Re-made (2 Cor. 5:17)—New Birth
A Vessel of Mercy (Eph. 2:10)—God's Workmanship
Wonderful Destiny (Rom. 9:23)—Prepared for Glory

342   Emblems of God's Word
(Jeremiah 23:29; Hebrews 4:12; Psalm 107:20)
A Fire to Melt—The Indifferent
A Hammer to Break—The Hard
A Sword to Pierce—The Self-righteous
A Balm to Heal—The Wounded

343   The Purchased Field
(Jeremiah 32:7-25, 44; Matthew 13:44)

Field to Redeem (Rom. 8:20)—The World is Lost
Kinsman Redeemer, v. 8 (Heb. 2:14; 9:12)—Christ
The Price Paid, v. 9 (1 Tim. 2:6)—Christ's Ransom
Title Procured, v. 10 (Rev. 5:7)—Christ's Authority
The Seal Affixed, v. 10 (Eph. 1:13)—Spirit Imparted
Evidence Given, v. 11 (Eph. 4:30)—Security Written
Waiting Time, v. 15 (Rom. 8:23)—The Present

344   In the Balances
(Daniel 5:27)

A False Balance (Prov. 11:1)—Man's
A Just Balance (Prov. 16:11)—God's
Actions are Weighed (1 Sam. 2:9)—Works
Men are Weighed (Dan. 5:27)—Persons
Christ was Weighed (Zech. 11:12)—Man's Estimate
God's Weights (Prov. 16:11)—His Estimate of Christ

345   God's Arrows

Of Conviction (Job 6:4)—Awakening Conscience
Of Deliverance (2 Kings 13:17)—Gospel Grace
Of Judgment (Ps. 18:14)—Hearts Hardened

346   Bible Lamps

The Professor's Lamp (Matt. 25:3)—Empty
The Possessor's Lamp (Matt. 25:4)—Filled
The Watchman's Lamp (Luke 12:35)—Burning
The Walker's Lamp (Ps. 119:105)—The Word
The Wicked's Lamp (Prov. 13:9)—Put Out

347 God's Books

Book of Election (Ps. 139:16)—God's Family
Book of Life (Phil. 4:3)—New Birth
Book of Remembrance (Mal. 3:16)—God's Witnesses
Book of Condemnation (Rev. 20:12)—Sinners' Works

348 Robes in God's Wardrobe

A Robe of Righteousness (Isa. 61:10)—For the Guilty
A Robe of Relationship (Luke 15:22)—For Prodigals
A Robe of Redemption (Rev. 7:9)—For Glory

SALVATION TRUTHS

349   The Salvation of God
(Acts 28:28)

Salvations's Author is Christ (Heb. 5:9)
Salvation's Cause is the Cross (Heb. 2:10)
Salvation's Proclamation in the Gospel (Eph. 1:12)
Salvation's Reception is by Faith (Eph. 2:8)
Salvation's Assurance is by the Word (Acts 13:26)

350   Salvation's Accompaniments
(Hebrews 6:9)

The Knowledge of Salvation, our Start (Luke 1:77)
The Joy of Salvation, our Happiness (Ps. 9:14)
The Wells of Salvation, our Refreshment (Isa. 12:3)
The Cup of Salvation, our Strength (Ps. 116:13)
The Hope of Salvation, our Prospect (1 Thess. 5:8)

351   Sinners, Sons, Servants

Sinners by Nature and Practice (Rom. 5:19; 6:17)
Sons by Redemption and Regeneration (Gal. 4:5, 7)
Servants by Call and Gift (Gal. 1:15; Rom. 12:6)

> The *First* tells our Ruin and Guilt
> The *Second* describes New Relationship and Position
> The *Third* relates to Surrender and Service

352   An Old Time Gospel Picture
(Psalm 49:7-20)

Redemption by the Blood of Christ (v. 8)

Resurrection by the Power of Christ (v. 15)

Retribution for the Rejection of Christ (v. 19)

> The *First* was Procured at the Cross (1 Peter 1:19)
> The *Second* will take place at His Coming (1 Cor. 15:52)
> The *Third* will ensue at His Appearing (2 Thess. 1:7-8)

353   Sin's Confession and Cleansing
(Psalm 51:1-10)

Sin Confessed before God (vv. 4, 5)

Sin Cleansed by Blood (vv. 6, 7-9)

Sin's Power broken by Renewal (vv. 10, 11)

Sin's Results annulled by Restoration (vv. 12, 13)

> Confession puts the Sinner right before God (Job 40:4)
> Cleansing sets the Conscience right with God (Heb. 10:2)
> Regeneration gives a New Nature from God (Eph. 4:24)
> Restoration brings into Communion with God (1 John 1:6)

354   Great Expostulations
(Proverbs 8:4)

God *Commands* Men to Repent (Acts 17:30)

God *Beseeches* Men to be Reconciled (2 Cor. 5:20)

God *Invites* Men to Reason with Him (Isa. 1:18)

God *Warns* Men not to Turn from Him (Prov. 1:25)

355   God's Love Toward Man
(Titus 3:4)

It is *Manifested* in the Gift of Christ (1 John 4:9)

It is *Commended* by the Death of Christ (Rom. 5:8)

It is *Believed* by the Receiving of Christ (1 John 4:11)

It is *Enjoyed* in the Spirit of Christ (Rom. 5:5)

356   What the Grace of God Does
(1 Corinthians 15:10)

It *Brings* Salvation to Sinners (Titus 2:11)
It *Saves* them that Believe (Eph. 2:8)
It *Justifies* all who Trust (Rom. 3:24)
It *Preserves* those who are Christ's (1 Peter 5:12)

357   What is Well-pleasing to God?
(Isaiah 42:21)

The Person of His Beloved Son (Matt. 3:17)
To Save all who Believe in Him (1 Cor. 1:21)
His People Accepted in Christ (Ps. 149:4)
Their Worship and their Work (Heb. 13:16, 21)

358   Things Not Seen, and Eternal
(2 Corinthians 4:18)

"Eternal Redemption," no Exhaustion (Heb. 9:12)
"Eternal Life," which has no Cessation (1 Tim. 6:12)
"Eternal Inheritance," no Deterioration (Heb. 9:15)
"Eternal Glory," which has no Decay (1 Peter 5:11)

359   According to the Power of God
(2 Timothy 1:8)

It is Exercised in the Salvation of Sinners (Rom. 1:16)
It is Experienced in Life by Believers (2 Cor. 13:4)
It is Manifest in Continuance in Faith (1 Cor. 2:5)
It is Proved in Preservation of the Tried (1 Peter 1:5)

360 From the Power of Satan Unto God
(Acts 26:18)

Sinners are under His Dominion (Luke 11:21)
Christ discomfited him on Calvary (Heb. 2:4)
Deliverance is Proclaimed in the Gospel (Luke 4:18)
Deliverance is Experienced in Believing (Col. 1:13)
Strength is Provided for Resistance (Eph. 6:10)
Final Victory is Promised (Rom. 16:20)

361 Deliver Us From Evil
(Matthew 6:13)

Redeemed from all Evil (Gen. 48:16)
Preserved from all Evil (Ps. 121:7)
Delivered from every Evil (2 Tim. 4:18)

Redemption is by the Cross (Eph. 1:7)
Preservation is from the Throne (Heb. 2:18)
Deliverance is by Christ's Coming (Rev. 3:10)

362 "Looking Unto Jesus"
(Hebrews 12:2)

As the Bearer of our Sin (John 1:29)
As the Pattern of our Character (2 Cor. 3:16)
As our Exemplar in Conduct (Heb. 12:2)

The First Look brings Salvation (Isa. 45:22)
The Continued Gaze imparts Transformation (Acts 7:55)
The Adoring View begets Discipleship (John 1:36, 37)

363 Coming to Christ
(Matthew 11:28)

Who are to Come? Sinners (1 Tim. 1:15)
How are they to Come? As they are (Matt. 9:13)
When are they to Come? Now (Luke 14:17)
For what are they to Come? Rest (Matt. 11:28)
What Results in Coming? Welcome (Luke 15:2)

364 Christ Is All
(Colossians 3:11)

There is no other Savior (Isa. 45:22)
There is no other Name (Acts 4:12)
There is no more Sacrifice (Heb. 10:18)

No Helpers in Man's Salvation
No Saints to Intercede on our Behalf
No Sacraments to add to Christ's Work

365   The Prince of Peace
(Isaiah 9:6)

He made Peace (Col. 1:20)—By His Blood
He speaks Peace (Ps. 85:8)—By His Word
He gives Peace (John 14:27)—In His Person

366   A New Creation
(2 Corinthians 5:17)

A New Creature (Gal. 6:15)—A Necessity
A New Birth (John 3:5)—Its Origin
A New Man (Eph. 4:24)—Its Result
A New Walk (Rom. 6:4)—Its Manifestation

367   Conversion
(Matthew 18:3)

Its Necessity (Acts 3:19)—Because of Sin
Its Production (Acts 11:21)—By Faith in Christ
Its Manifestation (1 Thess. 1:9)—In a New Walk
Its Rejection (Acts 28:27)—In Unbelief

368   Justified From All Things
(Acts 13:39)

The Meritorious Cause (Rom. 5:10)—Christ's Blood
The Receiving Means (Rom. 5:1)—Our Faith
The True Evidence (Titus 3:8)—Good Works

369   After This the Judgment
(Hebrews 9:27)

Predicted by the Prophets (Eccl. 11:9)
Announced by the Lord (John 5:30)
Testified by the Apostles (Rom. 2:16)
Assured by the Resurrection (Acts 17:31)
Recorded in the Revelation (Rev. 20:12)

370   The Gift of God, Eternal Life
(Romans 6:23)

Imparted in Believing (John 20:31)
Possessed by Believers (John 3:36)
Assured by the Word (1 John 5:13)
Refused by Christ Rejecters (Acts 13:46)

371   The Mission of the Son of Man
(Luke 19:10)

To Serve and to Give (Matt. 20:28)
Lifted Up as a Sacrifice (John 3:14, 15)
Raised as a Savior (Luke 9:22)
Glorified in Heaven (Acts 7:56)
Coming as Judge (Matt. 24:27)

372   Christ, A Sacrifice for Sin
(1 Peter 3:18)

It was an Expiation of Sin (Heb. 9:26)
A Death-sentence for Sinners (Gal. 3:13)
A Propitiation for Sin (Rom. 3:23)
A Peace-making for Sinners (Isa. 53:5)
A Purgation from Sin (Heb. 1:3)

373   Christ's Finished Work
(John 19:30)

Completed on the Cross (Heb. 9:14)
Attested by the Resurrection (Acts 13:29, 30)
Accepted in the Heavens (Heb. 10:12)
Preached in the Gospel (1 Cor. 15:3)
Believed by the Sinner (Rom. 3:25)

374   A Living Epistle
(2 Corinthians 3:2)

Living: Written with the Spirit (v. 3)
Legible: Known and Read by All (v. 2)
Lightbearing: Being made Manifest (v. 3)

The *Origin*, is Birth by the Spirit (John 3:5)
The *Manifestation*, is Newness of Life (Rom. 6:24)
The *Result*, is Men see their Good Works (Matt. 5:16)

375   Sin and Grace
(Romans 5:20)

Sin brought Ruin and Death (Rom. 5:12-18)
Grace brings Salvation and Glory (Titus 2:11-13)
The Spirit Convicts of Sin (John 16:8, 9)
The Convicted Sinner owns it (Rom. 3:19)
Grace Saves all that Believe (Eph. 2:8)
Grace gives the Hope of Glory (Rom. 5:2)

376   Great Joy
(Luke 2:10)

When the Shepherd finds the Sheep (Luke 15:5)
When the Sinner finds the Savior (Matt. 2:10)
When Salvation comes to a City (Acts 8:8)
When we Hear of others being Saved (Acts 15:3)
When all the Ransomed meet in Glory (Ps. 16:11)

377   The Uttermost

Christ Saves to the Uttermost (Heb. 7:25)
Wrath will come to the Uttermost (1 Thess. 2:16)
Retribution will extend to the Uttermost (Matt. 6:26)

1. All who Believe the Gospel (1 Cor. 15:4)
2. Those who Reject the Savior (2 Thess. 1:8, 9)
3. All who Despise Grace (Heb. 10:29)

378   God, My Savior
(Luke 1:47)

A Present Savior (Isa. 12:2)—"God *Is*"
A Powerful Savior (Isa. 19:20)—"A *Great* One"
A Personal Savior (Isa. 60:16)—"*Thy* Savior"

379   "Through Faith"
(Ephesians 2:8)

Faith in His Blood (Rom. 3:25)—Is Justification
Faith in His Name (Acts 3:16)—Is Deliverance
Faith in the Word (2 Tim. 3:15)—Is Salvation
Faith in His Power (1 Peter 1:5)—Is Preservation

380   Intents of the Heart
(Hebrews 4:12)

The Natural Heart (Jer. 17:9)—Desperately Wicked
An Impenitent Heart (Rom. 2:5)—Despises Warning
A Contrite Heart (Ps. 51:17)—Confesses Sin
An Opened Heart (Acts 16:14)—Receives the Word
A Believing Heart (Rom. 10:9)—Accepts Christ
A Purposed Heart (Acts 11:23)—Cleaves to the Lord

381   "Who Hath Saved Us"
(2 Timothy 1:9)

Saved according to God's Mercy (Titus 3:5)
Saved by God's Grace (Eph. 2:8)
Saved through Believing in Christ (1 Cor. 1:21)
Saved in Christ's Life (Rom. 5:10)

382   "Now the People of God"
(1 Peter 2:10)

A people Saved by the Lord (Deut. 33:29)
A people Set Apart for the Lord (Deut. 7:6)
People to be a Possession of the Lord (Titus 2:14)
A people Showing the Praises of the Lord (1 Peter 2:9)

383 "Went on His Way Rejoicing"
(Acts 8:39)

Rejoicing in a Trusted Savior (Ps. 5:11)
Rejoicing in a Known Salvation (Ps. 13:5)
Rejoicing in the Person of Christ (Phil. 3:3)
Rejoicing in the Word of God (Jer. 15:16)
Rejoicing in the Hope of Glory (Rom. 5:2)

384 Possessing Their Possessions
(Obadiah 17)

Take the Cup of Salvation (Ps. 116:113)
Lay hold on Eternal Life (1 Tim. 6:12)
Let us have Peace with God (Rom. 5:1)
Know the Love of Christ (Eph. 3:19)
Hold that fast which thou hast (Rev. 3:11)

385 Paul's Mission and Message
(Acts 26:18)

To Open their Eyes (Gen. 3:7)—Conviction
To Turn them (1 Thess. 1:9)—Conversion
From Darkness to Light (1 Peter 2:9)—Transition
From Satan to God (Col. 1:13)—Emancipation
Receive Forgiveness (Acts 10:43)—Remission
An Inheritance (1 Peter 1:3)—Possession

386 A Threefold Cord of Salvation
(John 6:37)

The Father's Gift to Christ—Our Election
The Sinner comes to Christ—Our Reception
The Saved kept by Christ—Our Preservation

    God will have all to be Saved (1 Tim. 2:4)
    Christ welcomes all who Come to Him (Luke 15:2)
    None are Surrendered who do Come (Rom. 8:35)

387 "All Power Is Given Unto Me"
(Matthew 28:18)
(The Word in each case means "Authority")
He has Power to forgive Sins (Matt. 9:6)
He has Power over Demons (Mark 1:27)
He has Power to execute Judgment (John 5:27)
He has Power to cast into Hell (Luke 12:5)

388 God Is Love
(1 John 4:8)
The Love of God Announced (John 3:16)
The Love of God Manifested (1 John 3:9)
The Love of God Commended (Rom. 5:8)
The Love of God Believed (1 John 4:16)
The Love of God Reciprocated (1 John 4:19)

389 "His Greatness Is Unsearchable"
(Psalm 145:3)
His Mercy is great to the Guilty (1 Chron. 21:13)
His Love is great toward Sinners (Eph. 2:4)
His Power is great in Deliverance (Ps. 147:5)
His Faithfulness is great in Providing (Lam. 3:23)
His Glory is great in Salvation (Ps. 21:5)

390 Vital Truths of Salvation
(Ephesians 1:1-13)
Chosen by God in the Eternal Past (v. 4)
Redeemed by Christ at the Cross (v. 7)
Evangelized by the Gospel here (v. 12)
Trusting in Christ for Salvation (v. 12)
Sealed by the Spirit for Possession (v. 13)
Receives the Pledge of Glory (v. 13)

391   Manifestations of Christ

To take away our Sins (1 John 3:5)—By His Blood
Destroy the Devil's Works (1 John 3:8)—His Power
To Glorify His Saints (Col. 3:3)—At His Coming

392   Bulwarks of Salvation
(Hebrews 10:7-17)

The Will of God (v. 7)—Planned It
The Work of Christ (v. 10)—Procured It
The Witness of the Spirit (v. 15)—Secures It
The Word of God (v. 17)—Assures It

393   Relations to the Lord

To Turn to the Lord (Acts 11:21)—Conversion
To Confess the Lord (Rom. 10:9)—Salvation
To Cleave unto the Lord (Acts 11:23)—Devotion
To Serve the Lord (Col. 3:24)—Occupation
To Be with the Lord (1 Thess. 4:17)—Consummation

394   The Power of God's Word

A Glass to Show the State (James 1:3)
A Sword to Pierce the Heart (Heb. 4:12)
A Seed to Quicken the Soul (1 Peter 1:23)
A Laver to Cleanse the Person (Eph. 5:26)
A Lamp to Light the Path (Ps. 119:105)

395   Great Deliverance
(Psalm 18:50)

Delivered from the Lowest Hell (Ps. 84:2)
Delivered from the Curse of Law (Gal. 3:13)
Delivered from the Power of Darkness (Col. 1:13)
Delivered from the Present World (Gal. 1:4)

396 The Name of Jesus
(Matthew 1:21)
Through His Name is Remission (Acts 10:43)
In His Name is Salvation (Acts 4:12)
By His Name is Life (John 20:31)

397 Threefold Crucifixion
(Galatians 6:14-16)
The Cross of Christ—The Savior's Atonement
The World's Crucifixion—Its Judicial End
The Christian's Death—His Separation from it

398 Righteousness and Strength
(Isaiah 25:24)
Christ is made unto us Righteousness (1 Cor. 1:30)
The End of the Law for Righteousness (Rom. 10:4)
The Believing Sinner's Righteousness (Phil. 3:9)
Christ is the Strength of His Own (Phil. 4:13)
His Power rests upon Them (2 Cor. 12:9)

399 Pentecostal Conditions
(Acts 1 and 2)
The Lord Ascends to Heaven (Acts 1:9)
The Spirit Descends to Earth (Acts 2:1)
The Gospel goes Forth to the People (Acts 2:14)
Saved Ones are Brought into the Church (Acts 2:47)

400 Carried and Cared For
The Lord's Continual Service for His Own
Found and Laid on His Shoulder (Luke 15:5)
Carried thereon all the Way (Deut. 33:12)
Upheld by His everlasting Arms (Deut 33:27)
Covered in the Shadow of His Hand (Isa. 51:16)

401   The Love of Christ

Its Everlastingness (Jer. 31:3)—I have Loved
Its Boundlessness (Eph. 3:19)—Passeth Knowledge
Its Surrender (Gal. 2:20)—He gave Himself
Its Service (John 13:1)—He Loves to the End

402   Dead Yet Alive

(Ephesians 2:1; Colossians 3:7)

Dead Toward God (Rom. 5:12; Col. 2:13)
Alive and Active in Sin (Eph. 2:3)
Christ Quickens the Dead (John 5:21)
He Redeems and Delivers from Sin (Titus 2:14)

These two Aspects of the Truth should be presented in their proper relations. Redemption is God's remedy for the one, Regeneration for the other.

403   Christ's Atonement

He was the Ransom (1 Tim. 2:6)
He is the Propitiation (1 John 2:2)
He shall be the Reconciler (Col. 1:20)

404   What Christ's Blood Does

It Looses from Sin's Power (Rev. 1:5)
It Justifies from Sin's Condemnation (Rom. 5:9)
It Sets Apart from Sin's Company (Heb. 12:1)

TRUTHS FOR THE ANXIOUS

405   God's Good Tidings
(Luke 2:10)

Gospel of Peace to the Troubled (Rom. 10:15)

Gospel of Salvation to the Lost (Eph. 1:13)

Gospel of Glory to the Fearful (2 Cor. 4:4)

> He made Peace and Imparts it (Col. 1:20; John 14:27)
> He brought Salvation and Gives it (Isa. 63:5; Rom. 10:9)
> He is the Lord and Giver of Glory (1 Cor. 2:8; John 17:22)

406   The Sinner's Discharge
(Isaiah 43:25)

Christ's Redemption Procured Forgiveness (Eph. 1:6)

Remission is Preached in His Name (Acts 10:43)

Forgiveness Proclaimed in the Gospel (Acts 13:38)

Justification is Assured to Believers (Acts 13:39)

Absolution is Enjoyed by Them (1 John 2:12)

407   Our Iniquities
(Psalm 90:8)

Iniquities Separate the Sinner from God (Isa. 59:2)

Iniquity Laid upon the Sinbearer (Isa. 53:6)

Iniquities Forgiven to the Believer (Rom. 4:7)

Iniquities Remembered no More (Heb. 10:17)

> The Sinner's Ruin and State *in* Sin (Rom. 5:12)
> The Savior's Death as a Sacrifice *for* Sin (1 Peter 2:24)
> The Believing One's Riddance *from* Sin (Ps. 103:3)
> The Blotting Out forever *of* Sin (Isa. 43:25)

408 Abraham Believed God
(Romans 4:4)

He Received God's Testimony (v. 18)
He Believed in God's Faithfulness (v. 20)
He Confided in God's Ability (v. 21)
He Enjoyed God's Acceptance (v. 5)

409 Saving Faith
(Ephesians 2:8)

Faith has as its Basis, God's Word (Rom. 10:17)
Faith has as its Object, God's Son (Eph. 1:13)
Faith has as its Assurance, God's Fidelity (Rom. 4:21)
Faith has its Evidence, God's Witness (Rom. 8:16)

410 Christ's Gifts

He gives Life to the Dead (John 10:10, 27)
He gives Light to the Dark (Isa. 62:2)
He gives Liberty to the Bound (Luke 4:18)

Life comes through hearing His Voice (John 5:25)
Life shines from the Written Word (Ps. 119:130)
Liberty comes in Using the Truth (John 8:36)

411 The Believing Sinner's Acceptance

"I will accept you with your sweet savor (Ezek. 20:41)

Christ's Sacrifice Accepted by God (Eph. 5:2)
Christ Accepted by the Sinner (John 1:12)
The Believing Sinner Accepted in Christ (Eph. 1:16)
His Person is Well-pleasing to God (Rom. 12:1)

The *Ground* of Acceptance is Christ's Work
The *Means* of Acceptance is our Faith
The *Position* of Acceptance is "in Christ"
The *Result* of Acceptance is Acceptability

412 The Results of Christ's Work
(Isaiah 32:17)

Its Results Godward is Righteousness (Rom. 3:25)
Its Results Manward is Peace (Col. 1:20)
Its Effects in the Soul is Quietness (Job 34:29)
Its Testimony by the Word, Assurance (1 Thess. 1:5)

413 The Gospel's Freeness

"Any Man" may enter in by Christ (John 10:9)
"Any Man" may drink from Christ (John 7:37)
"Any Man" who opens, Christ enters (Rev. 3:20)

414 For All Mankind

Ruin by Sin extends *over* All (Rom. 3:23)
Christ's Ransom was *for* All (1 Tim. 2:6)
Grace brings Salvation *to* All (Titus 2:11)
God's Righteousness is *unto* All (Rom. 3:22)

Human Depravity and Need are Universal
Christ's Ransom is All-Sufficient
Salvation by Grace is within Reach of All
Divine Righteousness is Offered unto All

415 Fear Nots

"Fear Not" (Isa. 43:1)—The Word of Redemption
"Fear Not" (Luke 2:10)—The Word of Peace
"Fear Not" (Luke 12:32)—The Word of Assurance

In this order, the Lord's message comes to, and is accepted by the soul. Redemption realized brings Pardon and Peace. Power comes through the Assurance of Divine faithfulness.

416 Three Ways

The Way of Life (Matt. 7:14)
The Way of Holiness (Isa. 30:8)
The Way of Happiness (Ps. 119:1)

Life is Entered through Christ (John 14:6)
Holiness is Sanctification by the Word (John 17:17)
Happiness is the Result of Obedience (John 13:17)

417   Christ All-sufficient

As Savior to Deliver (Matt. 1:23)
As Shepherd to Lead (Ps. 23:1)
As High Priest to Succor (Heb. 2:18)
As Lord to Control (Col. 3:17)

418   Full Salvation

Freely Forgiven all Trespasses (Col. 2:13)
Fully Justified from all Things (Acts 13:39)
Finally Glorified in all Fulness (Rom. 8:30)

419   Divine Power Exercised for Believers

To Save all who Believe (Rom. 1:16)
To Keep in Times of Trial (1 Peter 1:5)
To Sustain in Seasons of Weakness (2 Cor. 12:9)
To Strengthen for all Service (Eph. 3:16)

420   Results of the Cross

By Christ's Ransom (1 Tim. 2:6)—Release
Through Christ's Redemption (Gal. 1:4)—Deliverance
In Christ's Sacrifice (Eph. 5:2)—Acceptance
By Christ's Blood (Rev. 1:5)—Cleansing

421   The Way to God

By Reconciliation, we are Brought to God (Rom. 5:10)
In Regeneration, we are Born of God (1 John 5:1)
Through Resurrection, are to be with God (1 Peter 1:3)

422   Great Gifts

The Gift of God's Son (John 3:16)—To All
The Gift of Eternal Life (Rom. 6:23)—In Christ
The Gift of the Spirit (Acts 10:45)—Faith's Seal
The Gift of Eternal Glory (John 17:22)—Our Hope

423 Occupation With Christ

Beholding Him for Salvation (John 1:29)
Sitting at His Feet (Luke 10:39)
Listening to His Voice (John 10:27)
Leaning on His Bosom (John 13:23)
Following in His Steps (1 Peter 2:21)

424 All-embracing Promises

"Whosoever" is Saved by Believing (John 3:16)
"Whatsoever" asked in Faith is Given (John 15:16)
"Whithersoever," there is Preservation (2 Sam. 8:6)

425 Personal Decisions

"As for Me" (Josh. 24:15)—Life's Decision
"As for Me" (1 Sam 12:23)—Holy Resolution
"As for Me" (Ps. 17:15)—Hope's Anticipation

426 The Hand of the Lord

By His Hand (Acts 11:21)—Salvation
In His Hand (John 10:28)—Security
Held by His Hand (Ps. 73:23)—Support
Graven on His Hands (Isa. 49:16)—Remembrance

427 Good Security

None who Come to Christ are Cast Out (John 6:37)
No One is able to Pluck them from Him (John 10:28)
No Weapon can Prosper against Them (Isa. 54:17)
No Creature can Sever from His Love (Rom. 8:39)

428 Coming to the Savior

A Great Invitation to Come (Matt. 11:28)
A Grand Welcome to All who Come (Luke 15:2)
A Glorious Assurance for All who Come (John 6:37)

GOSPEL BLESSINGS

429 What the Gospel Brings

"Good Tidings" of a Savior (Luke 2:10)
"Rich Mercy" to a Sinner (Eph. 2:4)
"Great Salvation" by God's Grace (Titus 2:11)
"Eternal Life" as a Free Gift (Rom. 6:23)

Some Believe, others Reject the Message (Acts 28:24)
The Results Here and Hereafter (John 3:36)

430 Eternal Blessings of Believers

Eternal Life in Present Possession (1 John 5:13)
Eternal Salvation in Joyful Experience (Heb. 5:9)
Eternal Glory in Happy Prospect (1 Peter 5:10)

431 The Believer's Position in Christ

Accepted in the Beloved (Eph. 1:6)—One Standing
Complete in Christ (Col. 2:10)—One Reception
Joined to the Lord (1 Cor. 6:17)—One Spirit
A Member of His Body (Eph. 5:30)—One Life

432 Wonderful Security
(In Romans, Chapter 8)

"No Condemnation" against those in Christ (v. 1)
"No Charge" against the Justified (v. 33)
"No Separation" from Christ's Love (v. 35)

433 The Father

To the Father as a Sinner (Luke 15:18)—For Salvation
For the Father as a Servant (Matt. 21:29)—To Work
With the Father as a Son (John 14:2)—At Home

434 The Lamb

In the Book of Revelation
The Blood of the Lamb (7:14)—For Cleansing
The Throne of the Lamb (22:1)—For Rule
The Marriage of the Lamb (19:7)—For Joy
The Wrath of the Lamb (6:16)—For Retribution

435 The Words of Christ

The Savior's Loving Invitation (Matt. 11:28)
The Lord's Sad Lamentation (John 5:40)
The Judge's Solemn Declaration (Matt. 7:23)

436 Threefold Assurance

The Perfect Work of Christ (Heb. 10:26-28)
The Unchanging Word of God (1 John 5:13)
The Holy Spirit's Witness (Rom. 8:16)

> The Cross Assures of Sin put Away
> The Word Assures of Life Possessed
> The Spirit Assures of Sonship

437 Faith's Objects

(Hebrews 11:1)
It Looks to Christ Crucified, for Life (John 3:14, 15)
It Gazes on Christ Glorified, for Power (Heb. 12:2)
It Looks for Christ Coming, for Glory (Phil. 3:20)

438 The Holy Spirit, And His Operations With the Gospel

(1 Peter 1:12; 1 Thessalonians 1:5)
He Carries Conviction to the Conscience (John 16:9)
He Reveals Christ to the Soul (John 14:14)
He Imparts Life in Believing (John 3:5)
He Seals Those who Believe (Eph. 1:13)
He Strengthens for Life and Service (Eph. 3:16)

439   The Touch of Faith
(Luke 8:43-48)

A Case of Known Need (v. 43)
An Experience of Great Disappointment (v. 43)
A Result of Hopeless Despair (v. 43)
Hears of a Great Healer (Mark 5:27)
Comes to Him: Personally touches Him (v. 44)
An Immediate, and Enjoyed Cure (v. 45)
Faith's Touch, brings Divine Power (v. 47)
Confession brings Assurance and Peace (v. 48)

440   Past, Present, Future
(In Ephesians 1:7, 8)

Redemption, from the Past (v. 7)—Our Release
Acceptance, for the Present (v. 6)—Our Position
An Inheritance, in the Future (v. 8)—Our Hope

441   Spiritual Life

Its Impartation (John 3:5)—By the Spirit
Its Development (1 Peter 2:2)—Through the Word
Its Consummation (Rom. 6:22)—In Glory

442   Saved, Set Apart, Sealed

Saved by the Work of Christ, Believed (1 Cor. 1:18)
Sanctified by the Will of God, Obeyed (Heb. 10:10)
Sealed by the Spirit of God, Imparted (Eph. 1:13)

443   "My Lambs"
(John 21:15)

Gathered by the Arm of the Lord (Isa. 40:11)
Carried in the Bosom of the Shepherd (Isa. 40:11)
Led in Good Pastures of the Word (Isa. 5:17)
Sent Forth for a Time into the World (Luke 10:3)

MESSAGES OF WARNING

444 "Boast Not Thyself of Tomorrow"
(Proverbs 27:1)
Time is very Short (Ps. 39:5)
Life is very Uncertain (Ps. 90:5, 6)
Death may come Unawares (Job 21:13)
Salvation's Day is "Now" (2 Cor. 6:2)
God's Time is "Today" (Heb. 3:15)

445   A Man of the World
(Luke 12:16-21)
A Prosperous Man (v. 16)
A Progressive Man (v. 18)
A Self-seeking Man (v. 19)
A God-forgetting Man (v. 19)
Called by God a Fool (v. 20)
Entered Eternity Unprepared (v. 20)

446   The Barren Tree
(Luke 13:6-10)
Planted in a Vineyard—Privilege
Came Seeking Fruit—Probation
Cumbering the Ground—Uselessness
"Let it Alone this Year"—Longsuffering
"Dig About It"—Special Dealing
"After That"—Limitation
"Cut it Down"—Retribution

447   A Divine Warning
(Job 36:18)

A Divine Certainty—"There is Wrath"
A Solemn Warning—"Beware"
A Sudden Call—The "Stroke" of God
A Hopeless End—No Ransom Avails
A Changeless Eternity—No Power Delivers

448   Longsuffering and Judgment
(2 Peter 3:9-10)

The Scoffer's Question (v. 4)
The Divine Answer (v. 9)
God's Desire is Repentance (v. 9)
God's Longsuffering is Salvation (v. 15)
His Judgment is Sure (v. 10)

449   Bible Times

A Time to Die (Eccl. 3:2)
A Time for Judgment (Rev. 11:18)
A Time of Love (Ezek. 16:8)
A Time of Salvation (2 Cor. 6:2)

    May be used to set forth the Four Great Facts of the Sinner's Death and Judgment, and the Savior's Grace and Power.

450   Wrath To Come
(Matthew 3:7)

It is already Revealed from Heaven (Rom. 1:18)
It has Come upon the Jewish People (1 Thess. 2:16)
It Abideth upon all Unbelievers (John 3:36)
It is to Come on Christ Rejecters (Eph. 5:6)
Believers are Delivered from It (1 Thess. 1:10)

451 Hellfire
(Mark 9:47)

Its Location (Matt. 5:22)—Gehenna
Its Constitution (Matt. 3:12)—Unquenchable
Its Duration (Matt. 25:46)—Everlasting
Its Character (Jude 7)—Retribution

452 Sinners of Capernaum
(Matthew 11:20-24)

They Despised Christ's Works (Luke 10:13)
They Rejected His Words (John 12:48)
They Repented not of their Ways (Rom. 2:4)
Retribution was their Doom (Gal. 6:7)
Righteous Judgment awaits Them (John 5:30)

453 Refuge of Lies
(Isaiah 28:14-18)

Man's Efforts—"We have Made"
False Security—"Lies our Refuge"
Unreal Profession—"Under Falsehood"
Hiding from God—"Have we hid Ourselves"
Divine Judgment—"Sweeps all Away"
Deception Ends—"Covenant Broken"

REMARKABLE CONVERSIONS

454   Manasseh, the Murderer
(2 Kings 21:16; 2 Chronicles 33:19)
The Son of a Godly Father
Followed the Heathen in Idolatry
Desecrated the Temple of God
Shed very much Innocent Blood
Convicted of Sin by Words spoken to Him
Humbled Himself before God
God was Entreated of Him
Sins Forgiven, Results Remained (2 Kings 24:3)

455   Nebuchadnezzar, the King
(Daniel 1:1—4:37)
Conqueror and Captor of God's People (Dan. 1:2)
God speaks to him in a Dream (2:1)
He Confesses God's Wisdom and Power (2:47)
Sets up Idolatry, persecutes the Faithful (3:15)
Owns God, demands Allegiance to Him (3:29)
Warned of his Approaching Doom (4:23)
His Pride, Boast, and Judgment (4:31)
Humiliation, Repentance, Conversion (4:34)
His Confession and Thanksgiving (4:37)

456   Nicodemus of Jerusalem
(John 3:1; 7:50-52; 19:39, 40)
1. His Awakening, Conviction, and Conversion
2. His First Feeble Testimony and Discipleship
3. His Devotion and Identification with Christ

All who believe, are born again in a moment, but all are not immediately, or in the same measure clear as to their salvation, or in their full confession of Christ.

457   The Woman of Sychar
(John 4:1-29)
The Sinner and the Savior Meet
Her Confidence Gained and Conscience Reached
Her Sin laid Bare and Owned
Christ Revealed as Savior to Her
Christ Confessed and Owned by Her
Others Hear and are Led to Him

458   The Man Among the Tombs
(Mark 5:1-19)
The Demoniac and his Dwelling
All Efforts to Reclaim him, Vain
The Great Deliverer speaks the Word
The Powers of Evil are Conquered
The Man becomes Christ's Disciple
He "tells" and "shows" what Christ has Done

459   A Palsied Man Forgiven and Healed
(Luke 5:18-25)
A Helpless Cripple brought to Jesus
The Faith of those who brought him
The Greater Need met First
His Sins forgiven by Grace
His Body healed by Power
His Bed carried in Testimony

Pardon, New Life, New Walk, Testimony

460   Levi, the Publican
(Luke 5:27-35)

At his Employment the Call Came
An immediate Response is Made
He leaves All for Christ
He follows the Lord Openly
He welcomes Him to his House

       Here are the Elements of a genuine Conversion

461   A Woman of the City
(Luke 7:36-43)

A Pharisee invited the Lord to Meat
A Profligate Woman enters Uninvited
The Murmuring of the Religious People
The Parable of the Two Debtors
Unlike in Liability: Alike in Bankruptcy
Fully Forgiven and Loving Much

       Guilt admitted, brings Grace into Action

462   Zacchaeus of Jericho
(Luke 19:1-10)

The Lord's last journey through Jericho
A Man desires to see Him pass
Climbed up and is called down, hastily
Salvation came to him where he was
He received Christ, joyfully
He openly offered to make restitution

   The need of, desire for, nearness to, and results of Salvation received, are here set forth.

463   Lydia of Thyatira
(Acts 16:13-15)

A Devout Woman, far from her Home
Attends a Prayer Meeting at a Riverside
Gospellers declare the Lord's Message
Her heart opened, her ears listen
She receives the Gospel and is saved
Confesses Christ and receives His servants

464   Saul of Tarsus
(Acts 9 and 22; Galatians 1; 1 Timothy 1; Philippians 3)
Scholar, Pharisee, Zealot, Persecutor
Ignorant of God and of Himself
Sincere, yet a Persecutor and Murderer
Confounded by the Glorified Lord in Heaven
Sees Him, hears Him, is Apprehended by Him
Learns his Sinfulness, and Christ's saving Power
Confesses Him, Testifies of Him, Loses all for Him
Called to Serve, and Witness for Him
Devotion, Service, Suffering, and Martyrdom

465   The Jailer of Philippi
(Acts 16:22-34)
Prisoners sing and pray in Jail
God intervenes by an Earthquake
The Jailer alarmed and seeks suicide
He acknowledges his need and asks the way
A clear and definite Gospel Message
A fuller setting forth of the Word of the Lord
A Household believes and is Saved
Baptism and Works meet for Repentance

466   The Robber of Golgotha
(Luke 23:33-43)
A Criminal Suffering for his Crimes
A Scoffer Sneering at the Lord
A Sinner Convicted of his Guilt
He Condemns himself and Justifies Christ
He Acknowledges Him as Lord and King
He Asks to be Remembered in the Future
Assured of Paradise with Christ "To-day"

A clear case of sudden conversion, and of entrance to Heaven, on the ground of Grace alone.

467   An Officer and His House
(Acts 10:1-48)

A Devout, Praying, and Liberal Man (v. 1)
Needed to Hear the Word of Salvation (Acts 11:14)
All ready, before God, to Hear that Word (v. 33)
Christ as Savior and Judge Proclaimed (v. 42)
Remission Preached in His Name (v. 43)
All Believing, are Saved and Sealed (v. 44)
Confess their Faith and Discipleship (v. 48)

468   Idolaters of Thessalonica
(Acts 17:1-5; 1 Thess. 1:5-10)

A Clear Gospel from the Scriptures (v. 3)
The Power of the Spirit with it (1 Thess. 1:5)
Believers take their stand at once (v. 4)
Persecution by Religious Opponents (v. 5)
True Conversion, manifest to all (1 Thess. 1:6, 9)

469   Corinthian Sinners Saved
(Acts 18:1-11; 1 Corinthians 14:1-3; 6:11)

Christ Preached to the Jews (v. 5)
Rejection, Opposition, and Blasphemy (v. 6)
The Gentiles reached with the Gospel (v. 6)
The Message that they Heard (1 Cor. 15:3, 4)
The Power that did the Work (1 Cor. 2:4, 5)
Conversions among many Classes (v. 8)
Their Past and Present Condition (1 Cor. 6:10, 11)

470   Among Idolaters at Ephesus
(Acts 19:8-20; Ephesians 1:12, 13)

Three Months' Testimony and its Results (Acts 19:8)
A Cleavage and Separation of the Saved (Acts 19:9)
What they Heard, Whom they Trusted (Eph. 1:13)
What they Received and Enjoyed (Eph. 1:6, 7, 13, 14)
The Certainty of their Salvation (Eph. 2:8, 9)
The Evidences of their Conversion (Acts 19:18, 19)

TRUTHS FOR NEW CONVERTS

471   Acceptance

Acceptance *of* Christ (John 1:12)—Gives Life
Acceptance *in* Christ (Eph. 1:6)—Gives Position
Acceptance *by* Christ (2 Cor. 5:9)—Gives Reward

472   Union With Christ

As Members of His Body (Eph. 5:30)—Life
As Branches in the Vine (John 15:5)—Fruit
As Stones in the Temple (Eph. 2:21)—Stability

473   Steps in Christian Life

Turning *to* the Lord (Acts 11:21)—Converts
Following *after* the Lord (John 10:27)—Disciples
Testifying *for* the Lord (John 15:27)—Witnesses

474   The Christian's Inner Life

Its Strength is Secret Prayer (Matt. 6:6)
Its Food, Meditation on the Word (Ps. 1:2)
Its Atmosphere, a Walk in the Spirit (Gal. 5:25)

475   The Christian's Walk

In Good Works, prepared by God (Eph. 2:10)
In the Light, which is of God (1 John 1:7)
In the Truth, which is from God (3 John 4)

476 Abundance of Blessing

Abundance of Grace (1 Tim. 1:14)—From God
Abundance of Life (John 10:10)—In Christ
Abundance of Power (Eph. 3:20)—By the Spirit

477 Possessions in Christ

A Title that cannot be Nullified (Heb. 10:19)
A Life that cannot be Forfeited (Col. 3:3)
An Acceptance that cannot be Questioned (Eph. 1:6)

478 My Salvation

The Security on which I hold It

Procured by the Work of Christ (1 Tim. 1:15)
Assured by the Word of God (Acts 16:31)
Secured by the Spirit's Seal (2 Cor. 1:22)

479 Christian Duties

Keep the Heart (Prov. 4:23)
Guard the Ears (Mark 4:24)
Watch the Tongue (Ps. 112)
Guide the Feet (Heb. 12:13)

480 Relations to the Godhead

A Child in the Family of the Father (Rom. 8:17)
A Subject in the Kingdom of the Son (Col. 1:13)
A Stone in the Temple of the Spirit (1 Peter 2:5)

481 Christian Characteristics

(In 1 Peter, Chapter 2)

As Babes feeding on the Word (v. 2)
As Priests showing forth God's Praises (v. 9)
As Strangers in but not of the World (v. 11)
As Servants doing the will of God (v. 13)

482   Steadfastness

Stand fast in the Lord (Phil. 4:1)
Stand fast in the Faith (1 Cor. 16:13)
Stand fast in the Liberty (Gal. 5:1)

483   Continuance

Continue in the Grace of God (Acts 13:33)
Continue in the Love of Christ (John 15:9)
Continue in the Truth learned (2 Tim. 3:14)

484   Words of Cheer

"Fear Not" (Isa. 41:10)—God is *with* thee
"Fret Not" (Ps. 37:1)—God is *for* thee
"Faint Not" (2 Cor. 4:16)—God is *in* thee

485   Christ's Present Ministry

He Maintains us by Intercession (Rom. 8:24)
He Restores us by Advocacy (1 John 2:2)
He Cleanses us by The Word (Eph. 5:26)

486 The Believer's Relation to the World
(In John, Chapter 17)

Given to Christ out of the World (v. 6)
In the World but not of It (v. 16)
Sent into it to bear Witness (v. 18)

487   The Christian's Manner of Life

Live Soberly, Righteously, and Godly (Titus 2:12)
Live henceforth unto Him (2 Cor. 5:15)
Live Peaceably with All Men (Rom. 12:18)

488   The Believer's Testimony

Adorn the Doctrine of God (Titus 2:2)
Shine as Lights in the World (Phil. 2:15)
See that ye Walk Circumspectly (Eph. 5:15)

489   Good Company

God is *for* us (Rom. 8:31)
Christ is *with* us (Matt. 28:20)
The Spirit is *in* us (1 Cor. 6:19)

490   The Inheritance and the Heirs

The Inheritance ready for the Heirs (1 Peter 1:4)
The Heirs fit for the Inheritance (Col. 1:12)
Preserved by God for each other (Acts 20:32)

THEMES FOR SPECIAL OCCASIONS

491   Three Bible New Years' Days

Redemption (Exod. 12:1)—The Lamb Slain
Resurrection (Gen. 8:13)—The Deluge Dried
Rest (Exod. 40:34)—The Glory Comes

The Cross begins a New Era
Resurrection uplifts a New Race
Hope awaits the Promised Rest

492   Great Victories

The Victory of Christ in Redemption (Ps. 98:1)
The Victory of the Believer Now (1 John 5:4)
The Coming Victory of Resurrection (1 Cor. 15:54)

493   Bible Marriages

The Marriage of the Soul to Christ (Rom. 7:4)
The Union of the Believer with Christ (Eph. 5:32)
The Marriage of the Lamb in Glory (Rev. 19:7)

494   Birthday Rejoicings

The Birth of Christ the Savior (Luke 2:9, 10)
The New Birth of the Sinner (Acts 8:39)
The Coming New Birth of Creation (Rom. 8:21, 22)

495   Coronation Celebrations

The Coronation of the Christ as Victor (Heb. 2:9)
The Glorified Saints Crowned in Heaven (Rev. 4:4)
The Coronation of His Faithful Servants (2 Tim. 4:8)
Christ's Coming Coronation as King (Rev. 19:12)

496   Bible Farewells

The Savior's Farewell to His Own (Luke 24:51)
The Christian's Farewell to Earth (2 Tim. 4:6, 7)
The Sinner's Farewell to the World (1 Tim. 6:7)

497   Anniversaries

Mention Loving-kindnesses of the Lord (Isa. 63:7)
Forget not all His Benefits (Ps. 103:2)
Remember all the Way He has Led (Deut. 8:2)
Declare His mighty Acts to Children (Ps. 145:4)

498   The Death of the Saints of God
(Psalm 116:15)

They are His Own Possession (Titus 2:14)
They are already Meet for Heaven (Col. 1:12)
His Seal is upon Them (Eph. 4:30)
He Brings Them to their Haven (Ps. 107:30)
He puts Them to Sleep (1 Thess. 4:14)
He will bring Them with Christ (1 Thess. 4:14)

499   An Aged Pilgrim's Departure
(Genesis 25:8)

Called by God at the Beginning (Gen. 12:1, 2)
Obeyed the Call of Faith (Heb. 11:8)
Was Justified by Believing God (Rom. 4:3)
Enjoyed the Friendship of God (James 2:23)
Looked for the City of God (Heb. 11:10)
Went to be with God (Matt. 22:32)

500   The End

Christ loves His Own to the End (John 13:1)
He is with Them to the End (Matt. 28:20)
The End of the Godly is Peace (Ps. 37:37)
The End of the Ungodly is Destruction (Phil. 3:19)

INDEX

124 / Index